Capital: Getting It, Using It, Investing It

Finance for the Rest of Us

2nd Edition

Philip J. Romero

Printed in the United States of America.

ISBN 978-1-7322970-8-1

FUNDAMENTAL IDEAS IN THIS BOOK

- **Fundamental Idea A:** Time Value of Money—**Chapter III**
- **Fundamental Idea B:** Risk and Return/Diversification—**Chapter V**
- **Fundamental Idea C:** Net Present Value—**Chapter VII**
- **Fundamental Idea D:** Bond and Stock Prices—**Chapters XIV and XV**
- **Fundamental Idea E:** Capital Structure (Debt/Equity Mix)—**Chapter XVI**
- **Fundamental Idea F:** Efficient Market Hypothesis—**Chapter XVIII**
- **Fundamental Idea G:** Portfolio Construction (CAPM and MPT)—**Chapter XIX**

SUMMARY OF FUNDAMENTAL IDEAS AND APPLICATIONS				
Chapter	**Idea**	**Application**	**Formulas/Tips**	**Shortcuts/ Alternatives**
III	A. Time value of money	Discounting: converting future values (FV) to present values (PV)	FV = PV x (1 + DR)^N PV = FV / (1+DR)^N	
V	B. Risk vs. return	Discount rate (DR) includes risk-free rate (rp) plus a risk premium	DR = r(f) + rp	-Normal US equity risk premium is ~ 6 to 8% -Normal US junk bond risk premium is ~ 4 to 6%
VII	C. Investment analysis/ project evaluation	Net present value (NPV)	NPV = PV (benefits) – PV (costs)	-Payback (time until benefits = costs) -ROI (benefits/costs – 1)
VII	C. Sensitivity analysis	Redoing calculations for each of several scenarios	Distinguish scenario variables (that are uncertain) from policy variables (options)	Boundary conditions
V, XIX	B and G. Diversification	Correlations among portfolio elements	Distinguish systematic from individual risk	Individual risk can be mostly diversified away with 15–20 individual positions. Market risk can never be diversified away.
XIV, XV	D. Bond and Stock Prices	Valuing financial assets	PV of positive cashflows	Application of NPV (Ch VII)
XIV, XV	E. Debt vs. equity financing	Costs of distress; limits on leverage	PV of distress	
XVIII	F. Efficient market hypothesis (EMH)	Weak, semi-strong, and strong forms of EMH	Use indexing in efficient markets	Vast majority of active managers underperform their benchmark index
XIX	G. Modern portfolio theory (MPT)		ABC: alphas, betas, correlations	

Contents

I Introduction: Why Finance Matters

- *You have a fabulous idea for a new business, but you need capital to get it started: to buy equipment, rent office space, train employees, and advertise. Your bank is willing to loan you the funds, but at a very high rate of interest. Instead, one of the Shark Tank "sharks" is willing to buy a 60% share in your company. You could also grow the company much more slowly by funding it out of its natural cashflow. How should you choose which financing to pursue?*
- *You are the CEO of a smartphone manufacturer. Sales are great, so you need to build a new factory to meet growing demand. Your VP of Operations shows you a menu of several locations. Each has different costs and each can produce a different number of phones, so each will have a different rate of return on your company's investment. What decision rule should you use to make your choice?*
- *Your company has grown quickly by reinvesting all its profits back into growth. The stockholders are getting restless: their wealth is growing on paper, but they want to see some cash. They clamor for the firm to begin issuing dividends. Some are considering suing you. How do you decide whether and how much to pay your stockholders?*
- *It is 2008. Your aunt and uncle are 55 years old and have saved diligently throughout their careers so that they can retire in five years. Eighty percent of their investment portfolio is in stocks. During the year the stock market falls by almost 50%. They now find themselves 40% poorer—they have lost more than a decade's worth of savings. You are helping them determine how much longer they must work to build their savings back up. Must they work until age 70? 75? Can they ever retire?*
- *It is today. Your grades in college are good, so you are considering switching your major to a very rigorous subject that offers higher pay after graduation than your current one, which is less rigorous. You must make this decision at the same time you are applying for another year of student loans. Is it advisable to go into further debt to get a job so you can earn more? How much will your added salary help you accelerate paying off your student loans?*

Running a successful business requires knowledge from a number of disciplines:

- Marketing, so you can acquire and satisfy customers
- Operations, so you can produce your product and deliver to your customers efficiently (and keep your costs in line with what your competitors charge)
- Human resources, so you hire productive employees who pull in the same direction
- Management, so all employees (including in the CEO's office) are encouraged to act in the company shareholders' interests

- Accounting, so corporate leaders and investors make decisions based on accurate financial information
- Strategy, so your firm creates and exploits a durable competitive advantage

All of these are necessary for corporate success. Although most business schools teach each discipline in isolation, none of these can be successful unless all of them are. This is arguably most true about one discipline not mentioned above: finance.

The finance function in a business encompasses two key activities:

- Deploying capital: Determining which projects should be funded, based on criteria related to each project's contribution to the firm's net worth. In a typical corporation this is a *Controller* activity.
- Acquiring capital: Acquiring from debt *lenders* or equity *investors* the funds the firm needs to grow. In a typical corporation this is a *Treasurer* activity.

Many large firms establish a *Chief Financial Officer (CFO)* position who oversees each of these functions and acts as a financial adviser to the corporate leadership (the CEO and board of directors).

In addition, all individuals need to invest capital to meet their long-term goals, whether it's buying a car, putting a down payment on a house, or saving for retirement.

- The vast majority of businesspersons spend most of their careers in one of the above disciplines, or perhaps a few. They may simply assume that capital will always be available for growth and that investment decisions will be made sensibly. Finance may sound as interesting as watching paint dry. This is especially true if you aren't a "numbers person": you may rationalize your disinterest in finance.
- But in reality, **finance and accounting are the language of business.** They measure a business' success. They encompass the tools needed to allocate a business' scarcest resource (capital). If you aspire to have real success, you will need to make decisions using financial criteria and techniques. Even if you are a marketer, or a human resources specialist, or a public affairs expert, you will need to sell your ideas to business leaders; and their language will be finance. The imperative to learn this language is even greater if you wish to be a leader yourself.
- Your interests may not be in business—for example, you may wish to have a career in government or nonprofits. Even then, most of the resources you use will come from businesses. Businesses pay a large share of taxes, and they consume most government regulatory attention. Business owners supply most of the donations that fuel nonprofits. If you wish to assure that your public policies are effectively implemented, you need to understand how businesses

will respond to them so that you can communicate with some of your key stakeholders.

How This Book Is Organized

This book is intended to be a very top-level introduction to corporate finance. **It does not replace a traditional textbook; rather, it distills the essential concepts and ideas covered in detail in textbooks**. Its macro-organization has four parts:

- Part I covers the concepts and tools used to make capital deployment (business investing) decisions. The key criterion is how much the benefits of the investment exceed its costs. This is complicated because typically benefits and costs occur at different timescales (costs now, benefits later). Tools used include *discounting* to convert *future values (FV)* into *present values (PV)*. Investors subtract the PV of the investment's cost from the PV of its benefits to compute its *net present value (NPV)*.
- Part II outlines the options available to a business to acquire capital. These are of two main types: *debt* (loans) and *equity* (ownership). Firms constantly adjust their *capital structure* (mix of debt and equity), based on the tradeoffs inherent in each option.
- Part III introduces personal investing, describing the markets for *securities* (financial instruments): debt, equity, and hybrids of the two. It explains the efficiency of liquid markets and how that efficiency affects an investor's design of his or her *portfolio* of investments. These concepts apply whether the investor is a company investing its own retained earnings, an institution like a university endowment investing to support its beneficiary in the future, or an individual (like you!) investing for retirement.
- Finally, Part IV makes it personal: it integrates the previous lessons to illustrate how these concepts and tools can be applied to several common personal financial decisions, and it summarizes the book.

The words "concepts" and "tools" were repeated several times in the foregoing section. The core of finance is a set of tools—mainly mathematical formulas—used to make financial decisions. Students naturally focus on these formulas, which are challenging and require repeated practice to master. But important concepts—fundamental ideas—underlie each tool. If you don't understand the concepts (fundamental ideas), you may use the wrong tools. So each Part of the book ends with a summary. You can also find a meta-summary of the entire book on its first page.

How to Use This Book

The key to any learning is application and practice. This is true for any skill you learn, and most especially true if that skill is very unfamiliar—as finance likely is for you.

In the interest of brevity and economy, this book does not include the usual problems and exercises found in college textbooks. Your instructor will probably assign a more traditional textbook for these. Do not see *Capital: Getting It, Using It, and Investing It* as a substitute for a traditional textbook; they are definitely complementary. Instead, **use *Capital: Getting It, Using It, and Investing It* to introduce you to a topic and provide a 50,000 foot overview: its emphasis is on fundamental concepts, not analytic mechanics**. The first page of this book highlights the seven fundamental ideas herein. Look to the traditional textbook for more about the computational details. But recognize that you may lose the forest for the trees as you focus on the details, so come back to altitude by skimming *Capital: Getting It, Using It, and Investing It* again.

Most importantly, practice these techniques! Your instructor may assign you some problems. Treat them as not merely an academic obligation, but as an opportunity to cement your learning. Better still, seek out other real-world problems and mull over how you would approach them if you were their decisionmaker. The business news delivers a steady stream of such opportunities.

Finally, solidify your learning by producing summaries of what you have learned. These can be particularly useful before tests. Research has shown that learners who organize material in a form that makes sense to them perform far better than those who simply accept the form their instructor (and textbook author) delivers. Not only will employing this approach help you take responsibility for your learning, but it will help you retain much more of what you have learned long after the test. And that is the real objective: not to pass a test, but to gain a skill that makes you more valuable as an employee or entrepreneur.

In a nutshell:

- Focus on the big, fundamental ideas.
- Practice the tools that apply those ideas.
- Watch for opportunities to apply these tools to real-world problems, particularly if you are not a "financial type."
- Learn actively so that you have these skills long after your finance course ends.

II Why Firms Need Capital

Say you are interested in opening a bar. The location is on the ground floor of a new apartment building that will house five hundred college students. Many of them will want a nearby place to socialize and spend money. Sounds like a great business—right?

We will ignore that question for the moment, which boils down to: *Can you realize enough revenue from this business to cover your costs and leave an acceptable profit left over?* ("Acceptable," as we will see, depends on your other options.) Let's assume the answer is affirmative, and starting the business makes sense. But you need capital to start: few customers will come to a bar that lacks some basic features, like beverages, furniture, décor, and servers. These all cost money. (You can "pay" some people with promises, but only some, and not for long.) Therefore, to launch a business, you will need to acquire *capital*—you will need to court investors.

Some of the capital expenditures a small business may need can include (with examples for a bar):

- A space to serve customers (i.e., the bar): you can buy a building or lease one.
- Inventory: the beverages you will serve.
- Furnishings: chairs, tables, a physical bar, decor, and possible games to entertain your customers to encourage them to stay longer.
- Initial staffing: While most of your staff needs will scale with the number of customers, some staff are needed initially or you will not have any customers. No one will patronize an empty bar. You will need to spend money to recruit, select, and train that staff.
- The above only scratches the surface. You should think about similar capital needs for a business that interests you.

Fixed and Variable Costs

You may remember the difference between fixed and variable costs from microeconomics. *Fixed* costs are those that do not change as your firm grows (that's why they are called "fixed"). *Variable* costs are those that grow as your number of customers grows—as your firm *scales up*. In our bar example, the real estate itself is a fairly fixed cost—it does not change whether you have one customer or one hundred. By contrast, liquor or staff are pretty variable: you only need to incur those costs as (or just before) you add customers.

In real life the distinctions aren't quite so binary. Your real estate may be a fixed cost for the range between one hundred and, say, three hundred customers, but beyond three hundred you need to add real estate, incurring new fixed costs. Variable costs likewise don't scale perfectly with the number of customers: you need one bartender even if you have only one customer. And if you wait to add staff until your customer numbers expand, you risk being understaffed, making your customers wait, and driving some of them away. Similarly, you cannot wait until you serve your last margarita from the bottle to run to the liquor store to replace your tequila.

Working Capital

What the above implies is that a business needs funds not just for the major upfront *capital expenditures* (often called "capex"), which have useful lives of more than one year and will mostly go to fixed costs. It also needs capital to stock up on items it needs on hand so that new customers won't have to wait. These can be inventory, furnishings, or staff. Although a bar generally gets paid whenever a patron cashes out a tab, many businesses must wait weeks or months to be paid, and they need cash reserves to pay expenses until customers payment is received. If customers do not pay until sometime after a business incurs expenses, it need funds to cover the gap. Collectively these funds used for routine expenses are known as *working capital*. This is capital needed not as a long-term investment like capex, but to fund ongoing operations. Without it the business would have to inventory to sell or staff to serve customers.

Holding Fixed Costs in Check

Together capex and working capital needs pose a major hurdle to launching a business. In addition, all continuing commitments the business undertakes—such as a loan payment to a lender—add to its ongoing obligations and eat into profits. Not surprisingly, many businesses try to keep fixed costs and working capital needs as low as possible.

Many new businesses have a single employee—the entrepreneur/owner. He or she often does not take a salary, but instead simply takes whatever profits are left after paying all expenses. Many restaurants and small stores employ several generations of the family. Family members may not be paid at all to keep labor costs down.

Similarly, some successful businesses outsource (offer to outside firms) responsibility for key processes. From its origin Nike has designed and marketed athletic shoes, but contracted with other manufacturers to make them. Apple does the same with its electronic devices. This approach eliminates billions in capex for manufacturing.

Amazon changed retailing not only by being among the first to permit buyers to browse and purchase its offerings online, but by holding very little inventory itself. Instead, some vendors are responsible for shipping items to Amazon customers from their own warehouses.

If you have heard of the "gig economy," this is the reason. People performing "gigs" (like Uber drivers) are not employees, but rather independent contractors, to a firm. (They are sometimes known as 1099s, after the IRS tax form that reports nonwage income.) The firm avoids the fixed cost of labor. The firm may need to pay more for this flexibility, since the worker is taking a greater risk and will seek to be compensated accordingly. But it keeps fixed costs down.

Debt is a massive fixed cost. Individuals or companies who **leverage**—take on debt—reduce their financial flexibility. If you take out a loan for college, you are stuck with the loan whether college or not increases your earnings as you intended. The loan persists even if you fail to earn the college degree it was intended to pay for.

Does this mean debt is always bad? Not at all. If you buy a house that will appreciate 14% per year with a 4% mortgage that is eminently sensible—as long as you are confident you can service the debt (make the payments). This is in fact a classic **arbitrage** play. But for the moment, the more important point is that all businesses (and for that matter individuals) need to keep a lid on fixed costs. Debt is one of the most commonly abused fixed costs.

Forms of Financing

Acquiring capital is often called *financing* and is the responsibility of the corporate treasury function. Treasury is one of the activities under a corporate chief financial officer (CFO), as noted in chapter I.

The capital you seek will come from investors. With rare exceptions, all investors' goal is to grow the value of their investments. No matter how exciting your company's story may be, investors will be appraising you by asking: *What rate of return can I earn if I invest in your company? How does that rate compare to alternatives with similar risk?*

Debt Financing

The simplest financing is debt—a loan. Loans can come from individuals, from banks, or by issuing bonds. (Bonds are simply loans that are traded in securities markets.) An investor provides you a sum; you agree to pay that sum back at a specified future time. To compensate the investor for tying up his capital for that period, you also agree to pay him interest—a percentage of the principal—each year until the loan is due. Your payment terms may require you to make only interest payments until the loan's maturity, when you must also pay off the principal; or you may be required to make both interest and principal payments regularly.

Loans have first position among a borrower's liabilities. If the firm ever fails and must be liquidated, debt investors (lenders) are paid off first. (Stockholders, covered in the next section, are subordinate to debtholders.) Consequently debt has fairly low risk. As we will see later, this also means it offers fairly low returns. Hollywood rarely makes movies about glamourous bond investors.

Equity Financing

Stock investors are not lenders; they are owners. Issuance of stock to investors means that those shareowners collectively own the company's **net worth**—the value of its assets after subtracting the value of its liabilities (like its debts).

When a company grows rapidly, its lenders do not see added returns; all gains go to the stockholders. By the same token, when the company does poorly, lenders do not suffer (unless the company stops paying—defaults on—its debts); all losses go to the stockholders.

Hollywood does make movies about swashbuckling stock investors, because stocks are sexy and bonds aren't. Stocks' higher risks bring the prospect of higher returns, which are the makings of good drama.

"Sweat Equity"

New firms often try to pay suppliers in equity. It makes sense for the firm, since it has very little cash—aside from that provided by investors—until revenues begin arriving. The first employees may be paid in shares. Attorneys who work on incorporation documents, landlords, and even caterers or interior designers may be offered shares wholly or partly in lieu of cash. It can be a way to keep startup costs down, but it also sacrifices partial ownership. And sensible suppliers realize that many startups fail and their equity becomes worthless.

This is one of the reasons why many recent millionaires have been very young, like Mark Zuckerberg, who founded Facebook: while a college student. Likewise, Bill Gates dropped out of college to found Microsoft. Not only are teenagers and twentysomethings the most technologically flexible, but they have not yet accumulated significant personal fixed costs. They may be able to bunk on the floor of a Palo Alto group house and code twenty hours a day to launch a startup. Most of them come away with little but sleep deprivation and valuable personal lessons. But for those early employees of the handful of startups that grow fast, their equity can make them very rich very quickly. A 1% share of a billion-dollar company is $10 million, more money than most people make in a lifetime.

What Is a Corporation?

Originally all businesses were sole proprietorships, owned and usually operated by a single entrepreneur. Later, several entrepreneurs joined forces to create partnerships. But in general these forms of ownership have limits. The business is unlikely to survive the death of its key owners/partners. Also the business' growth is quite limited because its owners are responsible for any liabilities the business incurs. A customer who sues such a business can gain access to the owner's personal assets, like their house or their retirement accounts.

In the nineteenth century, the *corporation* became a new business form. Corporations are separate entities owned by shareholders, but those owners' liability is limited. Creditors can seize the business' assets but not the personal assets of the owners.

Corporations can exist in multiple forms that are each treated slightly different by tax authorities, such as limited liability companies (LLCs), B-Corps, S-Corps, and C-Corps, whose differences need not concern us here. The basic distinction is whether the corporate entity pays taxes at corporate tax rates or simply passes its income through to its shareholders, who pay at their personal income tax rates. Most household-name companies are C-corps and pay corporate income taxes. Individual shareholders pay personal income taxes on their dividends and capital gains.

Private vs. Public Businesses

The vast majority of US businesses—perhaps 97%—are in private hands: a single owner, or a few shareholders, own the business. If they wish to sell they must arrange the sale with another buyer; this is often known as a private placement. Such private sales can be difficult to arrange, time consuming, and incur significant fees from brokers or middlemen to facilitate the sale. As a result, investments in private firms are not very *liquid*—they cannot be converted into cash quickly or cheaply.

In contrast, shares of companies traded on major stock exchanges such as the NYSE (New York Stock Exchange) can be bought and sold whenever exchanges are open, with very visible pricing (i.e., it is easy to get a price quote). These stocks are highly liquid.

Stocks traded on exchanges are publicly traded, and the issuing companies are *public companies*. This is distinct from the *private* companies mentioned previously. In the United States and in most developed countries, companies can only "go public" if they accept considerable government regulation (by the Securities and Exchange Commission [SEC] for most US public companies). This allows the firm to list its shares on major stock exchanges, giving it access to vast numbers of potential investors. It also allows the owners to liquefy some of their shares in the company that previously were effectively locked up by illiquidity. Listing a company's shares is known as an initial *public offering*, or IPO.

Every company needs to decide on its *capital structure*—what mix of debt and equity it wishes to use to finance its capex and working capital. This will be a component of Part III. As an individual investor you can invest your savings in debt or equity instruments—or better still, in a portfolio with some of each, as will be discussed in Part IV.

For now, though, let us turn to the building blocks of finance, starting with the most basic: how finance can be a time machine.

Part I

Investing Decisions: Deploying Capital

III Fundamental Idea A: Time Value of Money (Finance as a Time Machine)

If you use loans to finance your education, you are already experiencing the "time machine" aspect of finance. You do not have enough cash to pay for your education as you experience it, so you are borrowing from a lender. You will pay that lender back—with interest—from your postgraduate earnings, which presumably will increase due to your degree. Using debt, you have brought your future earnings into the present to pay for a current expense. Your money has traveled in time.

You already are familiar with "forward financial time travel," more commonly known as compound interest. If you are willing to part with the use of your funds for a period of time—say, a year—you can lend it out and earn interest. Do so for multiple years and your interest compounds: you earn interest on your interest. When Albert Einstein was asked about the most powerful force in the universe, compound interest was his choice.

For example, $100 invested to earn 10% annual interest, and left in place to compound, will grow as follows:

YEAR	AMOUNT	GAIN FROM PRIOR YEAR	FORMULA
0	$100.00	-	-
1	$110.00	$10.00	$100 x (1 + .10)^1
2	$121.00	$11.00	$100 x (1 + .10)^2
3	$133.10	$12.10	$100 x (1 + .10)^3
4	$146.10	$13.00	$100 x (1 + .10)^4
50	$11,739.09	$1,067.19	$100 x (1 + .10)^50
Etc. (N years)			$100 x (1 + .10)^N

As you can see, the growth in the sum is accelerating, because interest is compounding. Einstein had the right idea.

The general form of the compounding equation relates our starting, or present value (PV), to its future value (FV):

$$FV = PV \times (1 + i)^N$$

where i is the interest rate (or growth rate of the balance) and N is the number of periods it grows at that rate.

Forward time travel is of course what all of us do every day. Finance also allows reverse time travel, where future resources are brought into the present (as with a college loan). This suggests that time is an important element of the value of resources. This is known as the "time value of money."

"Opportunities" in Time Travel

Many financial decisions boil down to versions of the following question: *If I give up $X now, will I earn more than $X later?* (As you will see, "More than X" isn't nearly precise enough. The specific amount above X that you will earn is a central concern.) No one will give up use of $X today to get only $X tomorrow. They seek a positive return: say, of $X plus 10%.

What rate of return is reasonable to expect? Whatever you can get for another investment of similar risk. (The importance of risk will be discussed at length in chapter V.) That return is the opportunity we sacrifice if our money is used for, say, Investment A instead of Investment B. Economists call this *opportunity cost*. The opportunity cost of a given investment is the return foregone by not using it for an alternative opportunity.

This has profound implications. As an example, aiming simply to earn a positive return—not losing money—in the stock market isn't a tough enough standard. The average annual return for a stock index fund has historically been roughly 10%. So if you've earned 5% annually over the last few years, do not feel so smug. You sacrificed an opportunity to earn 10%. The use of benchmarks—alternative rates of return—to evaluate investment strategies will be covered in Part III.

Time Value of Money

Money's time value can be illustrated with a simple example. Say your friend is scheduled to receive a sum of money in one year—for instance, when his lottery ticket, already declared a winner, pays off. He can document with certainty that he will receive $20,000 one year from today. But he needs money now. He offers to sell you his right to that bequest. What would you pay for it?

Certainly less than $20,000. Your first reaction is probably that you can't be certain that something won't go wrong and deny you the transferred bequest, so you need to lower your price to reflect that uncertainty.

That's an absolutely correct reaction, and we will take risk up in chapter V; but for simplicity's sake, let's assume that there is absolutely no doubt that the $20,000 will be forthcoming in one year. Is this asset—your purchased claim on the lottery proceeds—worth $20,000 to you?

Again, almost certainly not. Why? Because whatever sum you spend to buy this claim can't be used for some other productive purpose—to deposit in a bank, to start a business, or to buy shares in an existing business. If you buy your friend's promissory note due in one year, you lose the use of your money for one year. The lost opportunity—opportunity cost—is the return that you've sacrificed by failing to make the best alternative investment. Let's say that the alternative is to buy shares in the S&P 500 exchange-traded fund (ETF), SPY, which you expect will return 10% over the next year. Then your friend's note is only attractive if its expected return is at least as good.

We "charge" the proposed investment—your friend's promissory note, $20,000 payable in one year—for the opportunity that you are sacrificing to invest in SPY and earn 10%. We **discount** the expected $20,000 payout arriving in one year by a **discount rate** (DR) 10% per year to express that **future value** as a value in the present, or **present value**. Specifically, we can rearrange the earlier compounding (future value) equation to yield:

Present value = Future value/(1 + discount rate) ^ (number of years until payment)

PV = FV/(1+DR) ^ N

PV = $20,000/(1.1) ^ 1

PV = $18,181.82

Where *N* is the number of years until payment. So you should not pay more than roughly $18,182 for the promissory note. The *discount rate,* shown as DR, is the rate of return the investor could receive from investing in the best alternative asset. We used the example of the stock market, but others often use a less risky investment such as the interest rate on Treasury bonds. The discount rate chosen should reflect the lost opportunity associated with the most likely alternative investment. We charge that opportunity cost to this investment by discounting it to reflect the time value of money we are sacrificing by investing here.

Assets can offer either a single payment, like the aforementioned promissory note, or a stream of payments. Stocks differ from bonds or promissory notes in that they may provide a stream of payments in the form of dividends. These dividends will be paid on a regular basis into the infinite future as long as the company's board elects to maintain the dividend. Note, however, that not all companies pay dividends and, of course, sometimes companies suspend dividends or fail completely.

Accordingly, assessing the value of a stock based on those future dividend payments is a bit more complex. The present value of all the future dividend payments is the present value of each payment, added together.

To explain this, let's go back to the example of promissory notes: If you bought two promissory notes—one guaranteeing $20,000 payable in one year, and the other offering $20,000 payable in two years—the value of that portfolio would be the sum of the present values of each note:

PV note 1 (due in 1 year): $20,000/(1.1) ^ 1 = $18,182.81

PV note 2 (due in 2 years): $20,000/(1.1) ^ 2 = $16,528.93

Portfolio value (sum of each note's PV) = $34,710.74

The *intrinsic value* of any asset is simply the present value of all future returns. This is true whether the returns are a single payment or multiple payments, uniform in amount (as in this example), or nonuniform.

The math of discounting to compute the present value is straight-forward if the future payments are constant. A challenge is in estimating the future value cash flows, which is outside this book's scope. So we will illustrate valuing a share of stock with simple constant cash flows: dividends. (Dividend income will be a core source of stock valuation, which we will cover in detail in Chapter XV.)

Valuing an Asset

Say that you own a share in an electric utility company, Divco, which pays $1.00 per year in dividends. Also assume that your best alternative use of your capital offered a return of 12% per year. Then the value of the stream of dividends over ten years from Divco would be as follows:

Year 1: $1/(1.12) ^ 1 = $0.893

Year 2: $1/(1.12) ^ 2 = $0.797

Year 3: $1/(1.12) ^ 3 = $0.712

...

Year 10: $1/(1.12) ^ 10 = $0.322

The total value of this ten-year stream of dividends is simply the sum of these ten present values, or $5.65. If the only returns to shareholders were this constant stream of dividends for ten years, a share of Divco stock would have an intrinsic value of $5.65. If it traded in the market for $7.00, it would be overpriced. If it sold for $4.00 a share, it would be a bargain.

Note that each successive year's dividend is worth less in the present, because each dividend is paid further in the future. By Year 10, one dollar in dividends a decade hence is worth less than half as much today. However, dividends don't usually end after ten years. What if we extended payments further in the future? For example, a $1.00 dividend payable fifty years from now would today be worth as follows:

Year 50: $1/(1.12) ^ 50 = $0.003

... or less than 1/300th of its future value of $1.00

This discounting effect is stronger at higher discount rates (alternative rates of return) and further in the future. We'll elaborate on this point in the next chapter.

Long-Term Ownership of an Asset

You can see that if you extend the time horizon far enough into the future, the present value of a dividend then is effectively zero today. So an infinite time horizon won't generate an infinite present value, since beyond some time horizon the present value of future cash flows will be as close to zero as to be negligible. Still those future payments do have value, so how can we compute it?

Ownership of an income-producing asset means, in principle, that you will receive payments in *perpetuity*. (This applies, for example, to any stock: as long as the company survives, its owners receive its earnings.) Consider our earlier equation for a single payment N years in the future:

$PV = FV/(1 + DR) \wedge N$

We're looking for the sum of all these future values, so we can take advantage of the solution to the infinite sum

$$\sum_{i=1} \frac{1}{n^i} = \frac{1}{n-1} \quad \text{where } n > 1$$

And substitute (1 + DR) for n in the equation to get:

$PV =$ FV/([1+DR]-1) or

$PV = FV/DR$

The value of a perpetuity—that is, a stream of equal payments forever—is simply the payment divided by the discount rate. Thus, the PV of a perpetuity of payments of D each year is D/DR. In the Divco example, the present value of a share of Divco stock paying \$1.00 in dividends each year forever (assuming an12% DR) is

PV (Divco share) = \$1/.12 = \$8.33

So about two-thirds of the share's total value will be realized within the first ten years, since PV (10 years) = \$5.65, while PV (forever) = \$8.33.

Put differently, all of the dividends paid from years eleven to infinity are worth about \$2.68.

You can see that an annual payment many years in the future is worth much less than a near-term payment. Payments earned far in the future have a present value of essentially zero. This is why the cumulative value of an asset is finite, even if its returns will be perpetual: the sum of all of its future returns isn't infinity. This is why British consols perpetual bonds that never repaid principal but offered indefinite interest payments could be sold during the Napoleonic wars: the missing principal repayments far in the future would have a present value close to zero anyway. The bond's value depended solely on its near-term interest payments.

Using Spreadsheets to Compute Annual PVs and Cumulative PVs

Spreadsheet programs make it easy to perform repeated computations like these. In the above example we needed to discount a constant payment by a constant interest rate, varying only the number of years to be discounted (the number of years until the payment will arrive). Spreadsheets allow you to write a formula once, then copy it into multiple cells. The program can automatically update the formula. (Details depend on the program, so we will not describe the specific keystrokes necessary here. In Microsoft's Excel, a copied formula automatically updates unless you specify that you wish a particular input—a cell reference—to remain constant.)

Table 3-1 is an example spreadsheet for this type of computation. It illustrates changes in present values for a number of years in the future for a given annual payment—in this case $100—shown on the upper left. Several columns are shown for alternative discount rates, with the DR shown at each column head. The cumulative present value is at the foot of each column.

For this spreadsheet it was only necessary to write the present value formula once, then copy it down all the rows in its column and across all the columns in the table. In other cells the discount rate and specific year automatically updated. This saves enormous amounts of time and reduces the chance of errors from retyping the same formula multiple times. Note, however, that it is critical that you examine the original formula to be sure it is correct, lest you propagate the same error into every other cell. You can often spot error if patterns across rows or columns are not what you expect—e.g., displayed values don't change when they should, or they rise when they should fall.

Table 3-1

Spreadsheet for repeated PV computations							
Annual payment: $100							
DR:	0%	2%	4%	6%	8%	10%	12%
YEAR							
0	$100.00	$100.00	$100.00	$100.00	$100.00	$100.00	$100.00
1	$100.00	$98.04	$96.15	$94.34	$92.59	$90.91	$89.29
2	$100.00	$96.12	$92.46	$89.00	$85.73	$82.64	$79.72
3	$100.00	$94.23	$88.90	$83.96	$79.38	$75.13	$71.18
4	$100.00	$92.38	$85.48	$79.21	$73.50	$68.30	$63.55
5	$100.00	$90.57	$82.19	$74.73	$68.06	$62.09	$56.74
6	$100.00	$88.80	$79.03	$70.50	$63.02	$56.45	$50.66
7	$100.00	$87.06	$75.99	$66.51	$58.35	$51.32	$45.23
8	$100.00	$85.35	$73.07	$62.74	$54.03	$46.65	$40.39
9	$100.00	$83.68	$70.26	$59.19	$50.02	$42.41	$36.06
10	$100.00	$82.03	$67.56	$55.84	$46.32	$38.55	$32.20
10 year total PV:	**$1,100.00**	**$998.26**	**$911.09**	**$836.01**	**$771.01**	**$714.46**	**$665.02**

In this case the key inputs—the annual payment and the discount rate—are in bold (the 0% DR column shows the original, undiscounted future values.). This spreadsheet required the writing of only two formulas: the basic PV formula and the sum of PVs. Each was written only once and copied into all of its sister cells—the whole table for the PV formula, and all of the last row for the PV sum.

This brute force approach is the best way to perform these types of computations when you are first learning. Seeing every computation helps you check for errors and allows you to develop intuition about patterns. In the table above we would expect PVs to be $100 in Year 0 (since there is no discounting for 0 years), and to fall for increasing years or increasing discount rates. All this is evident, so the calculations aren't obviously wrong. Spreadsheets make brute force relatively painless.

Conclusion

Converting flows of resources into stocks—i.e., streams into lump sums—or vice versa, is very common in finance. (This is the "time machine.") The key challenge is to account for the time value of money: using money for purpose A makes it unavailable for purpose B. We account for this opportunity cost through the discount rate.

A given future value is discounted less if only a short time hence, or if the alternative rate of return being forgone—the discount rate—is low. By contrast, payments far in the future or that forego a high alternative return will be discounted very heavily. **The best way to gain intuition about discounting is to try it out in a spreadsheet**. Build your own version of table 3-1, and see how present values decline over longer periods and at higher discount rates. Understanding this will be essential in spotting biases in financial analysis by unscrupulous (or merely inexperienced) analysts.

IV. Time Value of Money Shortcuts

Brute force is an effective way to learn discounting and to check your work, and spreadsheets make it quite straightforward. But eventually you will seek shortcuts. This chapter mentions a few. They offer you a tradeoff: time savings for slightly greater complexity.

These shortcuts are most useful when you must make FV or PV computations for many years. Spreadsheets can ease this burden, but only up to a point.

The "Rule of 72"

Few people can make compounding computations in their head. There is, however, a shortcut that provides a close approximation: the Rule of 72.

This rules states that the time it takes for a sum to increase by 100%, or to double--e.g., from $100 to $200--is approximately the growth rate (expressed as a whole number) divided into 72. For example if your balance is compounding at 8% per year, 8% becomes 8, so the number of years it takes for your balance to double is 9 years: 72/8.

The Rule of 72 is never exactly accurate, but it comes quite close for single-digit growth rates and/or single-digit growth periods. You can use it as a check on your formal calculations, to help you catch errors.

The Rule of 72 works well for growth well above 2x. For example, If $100 has grown to $800. that represents three doublings because 8 = 2^3. The Rule of 72 will provide the time required for one doubling, so three times that long will yield an eight-fold increase.

The Rule of 72 is especially helpful for approximating growth rates or periods over long stretches of time. For example, you can approximate the annual growth rate for a stock that has risen in value 1000-fold over several generations. 1,000 is roughly 2^10, or ten doublings. If this 1000-fold increase required, say, 50 years, that would mean that the stock's value had doubled about every five years (50 years / 10 doublings). It had sustained an average annual rate of growth of just over 14% (72/5.)

Again, the Rule of 72 is never perfectly accurate. But you should always be prepared to double check your formal calculations with mental arithmetic. Since most people cannot make compounding calculations in their heads, the Rule of 72 is a valuable shortcut.

Perpetuities

An asset you own pays you for as long as it can make payments. That is why about two-thirds of American families own their homes. As mentioned in the previous chapter, an indefinite stream of constant future payments is known as a *perpetuity*. Perpetuities exist not only in the ownership of real assets like real estate, but also (rarely) for bonds. During the Napoleonic Wars the British government issued bonds that do not mature, but instead pay a constant interest rate forever, known as consols. (There have been proposals for governments to issue new consols to take advantage present historically low interest rates.)

The present value of the stream of payments from a perpetuity is 1/DR x the payment. So as noted in the previous chapter, a $1 annual payment made perpetually, discounted at a 12% DR, would have a present value of:

$$\$1/0.12 = 8.33$$

Delayed Perpetuities (aka "Annuities")

This formula assumes that the perpetuity's payments start immediately and continue forever. Often payments do not begin until a specified date in the future. The value of the stream must be reduced to reflect that delay.

Say that payments do not begin for five years. The perpetuity stream is adjusted by multiplying the above present value by the present value of the fifth year payment:

PV (perpetuity beginning in Year 5) =

Payment x [1 / DR] x [1 / (1 + DR) ^ 5], or

Payment x 1 / [DR x (1+DR) ^ 5]

Such delayed payment streams are commonly called *annuities*. You can contract with an insurance company to purchase an annuity: you deliver a lump sum known to receive a stream of payments in the future, such as when you are retired (known as deferred annuities). Lottery organizations often purchase annuities to pay off their winners.

Finite Annuities

The final shortcut combines the two above. Say you will receive an income stream immediately, but for a specified period—such as a bond that will mature. The present value of that stream is simply the difference between the two previous streams:

PV (N year stream) = PV (perpetuity) – PV (N year delayed stream)

If our income stream of $100 per year will last five years and our discount rate is 10%, the formula becomes:

PV (5 year stream) = $100/0.10 – $100 x [1/(.10 x (1 + .10) ^ 5)]

In this case, five years of $100 payments, discounted at 10%, is worth $379.08. Specifically:

PV (perpetuity): $100 / 0.10 = $1000

minus

PV (5 year delay): $100 / [.1 x (1 + 0.10) ^ 5] = $620.92

equals

PV (5 year annuity): $100 /10 – $100/[(1 + 10) ^ 5] = $379.08

This has wide application. For example, you can compute the cost of any term loan (e.g., a car loan) using this shortcut to see how much more the total cost of financing a car purchase will be versus paying cash.

Here is an example. You wish to buy a specific new car that costs $25,000. Your friendly dealer is offering you a loan requiring $500 per month payments for seven years at 5% financing. To keep it simple, we will compute annual payments of $3,000 (12 x $500). The total cost of the car under the terms of the offered loan to you will be:

$3000/ .05 - $3000/ (.05 x 1.05 ^ 7) = $77,359.12

So, the incremental cost to you of financing the car (vs. paying cash) is $52,359 ($77,359 - $25,000)--more than the twice the cost of the car itself.

Let's check our work:

PV (perpetuity): $6000/.05 = $120,000

minus

PV (7 year delay): $6000 / (.05 x (1.05 ^ 7)) = $85,281.76

equals

PV (7 year annuity): $6000 / .05 – $3000/ (.05 x 1.05 ^ 7) = $77,359.12

Conclusion

I personally prefer the spreadsheet/brute force method, because I can make repetitive calculations painlessly and examine my computations easily. But memorizing a few simple formulas— the Rule of 72, perpetuities and delayed annuities—allows you to combine them to compute the present value of many income or payment streams.

These tools have very broad applications, such as:

- Projecting the value of your portfolio many years in the future
- Estimating the amount you need to invest annually to achieve a long term target amount.
- Comparing annual growth rates achieved by different investments.
- The cost of a term loan such as a car loan, student loan, or mortgage
- The value of a fixed stream of payments such as an annuity or a bond
- The value to you of your future earnings if you stay or leave a particular job.

V. Fundamental Idea B: Risk and Return

You have decided to start a company, FlybyNightCo. To raise capital you issue bonds. (We will cover bonds extensively in Chapter XIV.) You choose to issue bonds that mature in ten years, meaning you owe only interest payments until you must return principal to the bondholders in Year 10. You check the markets and see that ten-year bonds issued by the US Treasury are offering 2.3%. So you set 2.3% as your offered interest rate and wait for the phone to ring with eager investors (bond buyers).

Weeks go buy and no one is interested. Why? You mispriced your bond, failing to account for risk.

US Treasury bonds are about as close to risk-free as exist. If the federal government ever runs short, it can make up for insufficient tax revenue by printing more money. FlybyNightCo lacks this option (printing money would be counterfeiting). Your company may run into trouble and be unable to service its debts: to make loan payments when scheduled. It is inherently much riskier than the government.

If an investor is offered a choice between a more risky and less risky investment at the same return, they will choose the less risky one. The only way for a more risky investment to attract investors away from its less risky competition is to offer a higher return than they do.

Finance types break risk into two tiers:

- There is a base interest rate offered by the least risky investments, usually termed the *"risk-free rate."* The rate on very short-term treasuries is generally used as a proxy for the risk free rate.
- Other investments must offer a *risk premium* over and above the risk-free rate to attract investors. Risk premia vary across issuers of differing riskiness.

Risk premia vary by the type of investment. Even long-term treasuries can offer a modest risk premium, because the later the maturity, the more opportunities for surprises. Corporate bonds offer a risk premium over government bonds, because corporations rely on uncertain sales for income to service their debts, while governments can coerce tax revenues from their citizens. Rating agencies like Standard & Poors (S&P), Moody's, or Fitch evaluate bond issuers' ability to service their debts and grade them (AAA, BBB, etc.). Lower-rated issuers typically must offer a higher risk premium than AAA issuers. Bonds graded below BBB are considered "speculative" or "non-investment grade," also known as "junk bonds"; their interest rates are usually several percent above investment grade issuers.

Investments can be arrayed graphically in a risk/return space. Conventionally risk is measured by the volatility of periodic returns on the X-axis and average return on the Y-axis. A generic version of this plot is in figure 5-1. The specific location of each asset class is only approximate, because each can change over time.

Figure 5-1

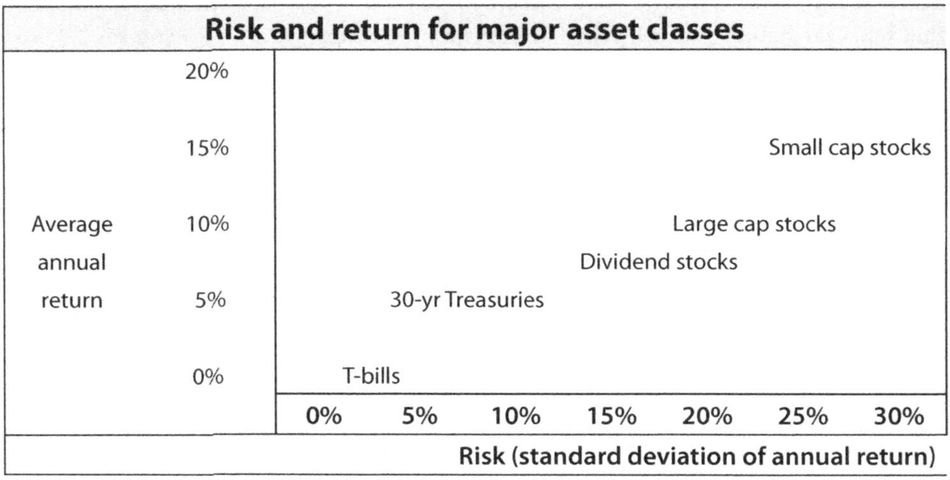

Again, do not take this graph too literally, but its basic message is clear: investors cannot aspire to increased returns unless they are willing to take on increased risk. "No pain, no gain" isn't only in the gym. (Chapter XIX will mention measures to assess whether an investor's increased risk is being adequately compensated by increased return.)

Risk and the Discount Rate

When you discount any investment, you must choose a discount rate based on that investment's riskiness. Your discount rate should be the rate of return offered by an alternative investment with similar risk to yours. FlybyNightCo's discount rate will be considerably higher than that of a AAA issuer to account for the significant risk premium it must offer.

All of the above is not limited to bonds. It applies even more strongly to equity investments. Remember that because shareholders are behind bondholders in a corporate liquidation, they will require a risk premium to compensate them. The equity risk premium is smallest for the largest and least risky companies, but never zero. Bond risk premiums generally run between 1 and 6%, based on the bond's issuer, rating, and maturity. Equity risk premiums run between about 5 and 8%. Each of these are spreads above the rate of return on a riskless asset, usually proxied by short-term treasuries. Spreads can explode upwards when investors are skittish, such as when a recession threatens.

This can give any present value estimate a somewhat arbitrary cast, because the choice of discount rate inevitably requires judgment. Judging which alternative investment has the most similar risk will always be subjective.

But the choice of discount rate has major implications. A higher discount rate will by definition significantly lower the present value of the benefits of an investment. Compare columns in table 3-1 for an example. This effect is magnified if the benefits occur well in the future. Changing the discount rate typically only affects an investment's benefits, with little effect on its costs, for reasons that will be apparent in the next chapter.

VI. Evaluating Investments: Common but Inferior Measures

Investing is fundamentally the act of expending resources now (incurring costs) to build or buy something that will produce more resources later (enjoy benefits). **Investments are mainly evaluated on their return—the margin by which their benefits exceed their costs**. As you will see, simply earning a positive return (having more benefits than costs) isn't enough if other investments can produce a greater margin of benefits over costs.

The next chapter will introduce the main metric finance specialists use to evaluate an investment: its *net present value* (net of benefits minus costs), or NPV. This chapter offers some preliminaries in order to make NPV more intuitive.

The Basic Framework

Fig. 6-1 shows the basic framework for evaluating any investment, commonly known as a **cashflow diagram**. Costs are in the bottom row and benefits in the top row, arrayed year-by-year.

Laying out the basic, undiscounted cashflows is the core challenge of any investment analysis. Students may receive this as a given in class exercises, but professionals know that getting these right so they describe the real decision problem is essential.

Figure 6-1

Cashflow diagram (undiscounted FV cashflows)								
		+$25	$25	$25	$25	$25	$25	$55
YEAR	0	1	2	3	4	5	6	7
	-$100					(Terminal value: $55)		

This sequence of cashflows is like that for a typical real asset investment: the investor lays out $100 today, and in exchange receives annual payments of $25 for seven years. She can sell the depreciated asset for $30 in the seventh year, so that year's cashflow is $25 + $30 = $55.

Is this a good investment? Let's look at a few simple ways to evaluate these cashflows.

Payback

The basic trajectory over time of an investment is: spend money now, get more money later. The sooner "later" comes, the better, under the thinking of the payback criterion. It computes: How soon do I get my original investment back?

Payback is:

Years until Sum(benefits) = Sum(costs)

In figure 6-1, payback is at the end of the fourth year—that is when the positive cashflows equal the initial investment (negative cashflow). Any amount received thereafter is "profit"—positive return.

Payback assumes that there are continuing positive cashflows beyond the payback date—that date is when the positive returns kick in. In such a situation, the sooner the asset pays back the original investment, the greater its total return will be, everything else being equal.

But payback ignores the timing and magnitude of the post-payback cashflows. Pretend that as an alternative to the investment in figure 6-1 you could invest the same $100 to receive the following positive cashflows: $50 in each of Years 1 and 2, and nothing thereafter. Would you prefer this investment? Not likely: although its payback is two years instead of four for figure 6-1, the only "return" you earn is getting your capital back. There is no "profit" at all. Payback ignores the amount and timing of any cashflows beyond the payback date.

Return on Investment (ROI)

We invest money now to earn more dollars later. So the margin by which our expected positive cashflow exceeds our outlay (negative cashflow) represents our return. The formula is:

Return on investment (ROI) = [Sum of Benefits (positive cashflows) / Sum of Costs (negative cashflows)] – 1

An asset that only just paid back its investment would have an ROI of zero, because benefits would just equal costs. ROI measures the excess return (profit) after you've paid back your initial investment; that's why we subtract 1.

In figure 6-1, the ROI for the seven years shown is: $205 / $100 – 1 = 105%.

ROI certainly sounds like a reasonable measure. But it begs several questions. One is: For what period should you measure cashflows? If an asset generates positive cashflows after its payback period, then the longer you measure these cashflows, the higher its ROI. This suggests another issue: ROI doesn't account for the time value of money—a dollar of cashflow is valued the same regardless of when it occurs. Should returns that come, say, twenty years after the initial investment really count the same as returns that come two years afterward?

Conclusion: Shortcuts are Fine as Rules of Thumb; Inferior as Formal Evaluation Measures

As noted earlier, the Rule of 72 is never exactly accurate, and comes closest for relatively low growth rates or compounding periods. You can use it to check your computations to catch wild errors, but it should never substitute for the real thing. It is, however, very helpful for quickly producing approximate answers.

Payback and ROI are used quite often in casual business conversations, and they have their place as simple rules of thumb. If I have a choice between two otherwise identical investments, it is probably reasonable to choose the one with a higher ROI, or a shorter payback. But in the real world it is very uncommon that everything else is identical. Investment A may pay back later, but in much higher amounts. Investment B may pay back more in the early years, but depreciate the asset more so it has a near-zero salvage value. Investment C may pay less and have a later payback year, but continue paying for many more years than A or B. A better method, described in the next chapter, accounts for such differences.

Both payback and ROI are easy measures, to compute, but flawed.

- Payback ignores all cashflows after the payback date. It assumes that they will be positive post-payback, and that therefore the investment will be profitable (have a positive return). But it does not measure that profitability.
- ROI ignores the timing of positive cashflows. An investment with a high ROI whose returns come far in the future doesn't account for that timing. In reality, we may prefer lower returns that come sooner.

Each of these simple measures has utility, and to some degree they complement each other. Payback captures the timing of returns, and ROI captures their (undiscounted) magnitude. But there is a better measure—the gold standard of investment analysis—that we will cover in the next chapter.

VII Fundamental Idea C: Net Present Value

The standard measure of an investment's advisability is its net present value, or NPV. **NPV simply computes the present value of each of the investment's positive and negative cashflows and nets them against each other:**

NPV = PV (Benefits) – PV (Costs)

The investment's NPV is the amount by which its returns exceed its costs, *accounting for the time value of money.* Differences in the timing of cashflows are addressed by discounting each cashflow into present value terms. Once each cashflow is expressed this way, they can be added together. See chapter III for a refresher.

Like ROI, NPV measures the excess return the investor earns over and above her costs. Unlike ROI, NPV discounts those returns to account for the time value of money--later returns are worth less than earlier ones.

Put simplistically, an investment is worth making if its NPV is positive—that is, if its discounted benefits exceed its discounted costs. The discount rate is the best rate of return available for alternative investments of similar risk.

Figure 7-1 offers an example. The cashflow trajectory is very similar to most bonds: we invest $100 today, earn $5 per year in interest payments for nine years, then earn the final $5 in interest plus get our $100 principal back in Year 10.

Figure 7-1

Cashflow diagram: Bond-like investment (undiscounted FVs)											
		+$5	$5	$5	$5	$5	$5	$5	$5	$5	$105
											(Receive $100 principal, plus $5 interest)
YEAR	0	1	2	3	4	5	6	7	8	9	10
	-$100 (Invest $100)										

Table 7-1 shows these cashflows for several different discount rates.

Table 7-1

		Discounted cashflows (PVs) for bond-like investment					
		Discount rate					
		0%	5%	10%	15%	20%	50%
	YEAR						
	0	-100	-100.00	-100.00	-100.00	-100.00	-100.00
	1	5	4.76	4.55	4.35	4.17	3.33
	2	5	4.54	4.13	3.78	3.47	2.22
	3	5	4.32	3.76	3.29	2.89	1.48
	4	5	4.11	3.42	2.86	2.41	0.99
	5	5	3.92	3.10	2.49	2.01	0.66
	6	5	3.73	2.82	2.16	1.67	0.44
	7	5	3.55	2.57	1.88	1.40	0.29
	8	5	3.38	2.33	1.63	1.16	0.20
	9	5	3.22	2.12	1.42	0.97	0.13
	10	105	64.46	40.48	25.95	16.96	1.82
	NPV	**50.00**	**0.00**	**-30.72**	**-50.19**	**-62.89**	**-88.44**
Benefits	PV (Yrs 1-10)	150.00	100.00	69.28	49.81	37.11	11.56
Costs	PV (Yr 0)	-100.00	-100.00	-100.00	-100.00	-100.00	-100.00

Inspect this table carefully to help you develop your intuition regarding the NPV measure. Undiscounted cashflows—the same as those in figure 7-1—are shown in the 0% discount rate column. If we ignore the time value of money (which a 0% discount rate does), the investment earns $50 more than its cost—a $50 NPV. Since the investment cost $100, this is equivalent to a 50% ROI over this 10-year period. Each column to the right of the 0% column shows those same cashflows, discounted at the specified DR for the same number of years.

NPV is simply the sum of all of the cashflows in a column: total benefits minus total costs, each discounted to their present values. The rows directly below the NPV show those benefits and costs separately to make the sum easier to follow. While the NPV for the undiscounted cashflows (i.e., a DR of 0%) is positive at $50, the investment looks less attractive once we begin to discount. At a 5% DR the NPV is zero—benefits just equal costs. At higher DRs, NPV becomes negative, and increasingly negative as the DR escalates.

This makes sense after a bit of thought. Regardless of the discount rate, the discounted cost of our investment in Year 0 doesn't change because it happens in the present. But higher DRs magnify the discount of each of the positive cashflows (benefits). As you can see, the magnified discounting most affects the later cashflows. At a 50% discount rate, the Year 9 payment is worth about 1/25th of the Year 1 payment ($0.13 vs. $3.33), because it is discounted for eight additional years.

For this investment, it appears that any discount rate equal or greater than 5% will render a negative NPV and cause us to reject the investment. This isn't surprising given that the cashflow structure is that of a ten-year 5% bond. So in this context, "rate of return" can mean the discount rate at which NPV equals zero. This idea will will be explored further in the next chapter.

NPV is the single most important tool in finance, so the next section offers a few examples.

Example: The NPV of College

Table 7-2 uses the same format as the previous table for an investment with quite different cashflows.

The difference between consumption and investment is the sign of the cashflows. When you spend on a consumption item such as an article of clothing or a video, it does not generate any positive cashflows to offset your negative cashflow for the purchase. Investments are, by definition, items that have at least a reasonable chance of producing more cash than they consume.

Students (and their parents, and scholarship donors) spend tens to hundreds of thousands of dollars on a college education, in the belief that it is an investment. But is college a good investment?

We will examine two possible college experiences. Assume that in each instance a college degree costs $15,000 per year and the student can complete it in four years (both optimistic assumptions). Student A majors in mathematics and enters a career in business, first as an actuary and later as an insurance executive. Student B majors in film studies, becomes an independent film director and later a film critic for an e-zine. Below are the cashflows for the years of college and their post-college career (forty-five years combined). All amounts are adjusted for inflation; that is, they are expressed in terms of the purchasing power of a late 2010s dollar.

The cashflows shown really underestimate the differences between the student's options. The math major graduates into a $70,000-per-year job. The film studies major graduates into a $30,000-per-year job. To keep the example simple, we assume that earnings remain constant for all three options: high school only, math major, and film studies major—even though in reality several of these may fall behind inflation over time. Table 7-2 summarizes these options, with Years 11 through 39 omitted for space reasons.

Table 7-2

NPV of alternative college degrees (All dollar amounts in 000s)					
	Undiscounted (DR = 0%)				
	High School only	College Options			
		Student A Math	A's difference vs. HS	Student B Film Studies	B's difference vs. HS
YEAR					
0	$25.00	-$15.00	**-$40.00**	-$15.00	**-$40.00**
1	$25.00	-$15.00	**-$40.00**	-$15.00	**-$40.00**
2	$25.00	-$15.00	**-$40.00**	-$15.00	**-$40.00**
3	$25.00	-$15.00	**-$40.00**	-$15.00	**-$40.00**
4	$25.00	$70.00	**$45.00**	$30.00	**$5.00**
5	$25.00	$70.00	**$45.00**	$30.00	**$5.00**
6	$25.00	$70.00	**$45.00**	$30.00	**$5.00**
7	$25.00	$70.00	**$45.00**	$30.00	**$5.00**
8	$25.00	$70.00	**$45.00**	$30.00	**$5.00**
9	$25.00	$70.00	**$45.00**	$30.00	**$5.00**
10	$25.00	$70.00	**$45.00**	$30.00	**$5.00**
Years 11 through 39 omitted for brevity					
40	$25.00	$70.00	**$45.00**	$30.00	**$5.00**
41	$25.00	$70.00	**$45.00**	$30.00	**$5.00**
42	$25.00	$70.00	**$45.00**	$30.00	**$5.00**
43	$25.00	$70.00	**$45.00**	$30.00	**$5.00**
44	$25.00	$70.00	**$45.00**	$30.00	**$5.00**
45	$25.00	$70.00	**$45.00**	$30.00	**$5.00**
NPV (DR=0%)			**$1,730.00**		**$50.00**
PV (benefits)			**$1,890.00**		**$210.00**
PV (costs)			**-$160.00**		**-$160.00**

Table 7-2 *Continued*

NPV of alternative college degrees (All dollar amounts in 000s)					
	Discounted at 6% DR				
	High School only	College Options			
		Student A Math	A's difference vs. HS (PVs)	Student B Film Studies	B's difference vs. HS (PVs)
YEAR					
0	$25.00	-$15.00	**-$40.00**	-$15.00	**-$40.00**
1	$25.00	-$15.00	**-$38.00**	-$15.00	**-$38.00**
2	$25.00	-$15.00	**-$36.00**	-$15.00	**-$36.00**
3	$25.00	-$15.00	**-$34.00**	-$15.00	**-$34.00**
4	$25.00	$70.00	**$36.00**	$30.00	**$4.00**
5	$25.00	$70.00	**$34.00**	$30.00	**$4.00**
6	$25.00	$70.00	**$32.00**	$30.00	**$4.00**
7	$25.00	$70.00	**$30.00**	$30.00	**$3.00**
8	$25.00	$70.00	**$28.00**	$30.00	**$3.00**
9	$25.00	$70.00	**$27.00**	$30.00	**$3.00**
10	$25.00	$70.00	**$25.00**	$30.00	**$3.00**
Years 11 through 39 omitted for brevity					
40	$25.00	$70.00	**$4.00**	$30.00	**$0.00**
41	$25.00	$70.00	**$4.00**	$30.00	**$0.00**
42	$25.00	$70.00	**$4.00**	$30.00	**$0.00**
43	$25.00	$70.00	**$4.00**	$30.00	**$0.00**
44	$25.00	$70.00	**$3.00**	$30.00	**$0.00**
45	$25.00	$70.00	**$3.00**	$30.00	**$0.00**
NPV			**$428.00**		**-$83.00**
PV (benefits)			**$575.00**		**$64.00**
PV (costs)			**-$147.00**		**-$147.00**

The students' baseline earnings expectations (the status quo) without a college degree are in the first column, "High school only": a minimum wage job earning about $11 per hour, or $25,000 per year. The assumption of no salary erosion over time is generous, since real wages for those with only a high school degree have been slipping about 2 to 3% behind inflation each year. The next group of columns shows expected real earnings under the two alternative career paths shown. Both college students spend $15K per year for four years for college, then their earnings progress on radically different trajectories, starting in Year 4 at $70K for the math major and $30K for the film studies major. Again, this example assumes no change in real earnings over time through a 40+ year career, to keep it simple.

The center columns in bold show the cashflows used in NPV computations: the difference in cashflows for each major vs. a high school degree. Undiscounted college is a no-brainer—each lifetime NPV is positive: the film studies major earns $50K more than his costs, while the math major earns $1.73 million. These are the kinds of figures often cited in university propaganda.

But the picture changes when we account for the time value of money. In this case we use a 6% discount rate, similar to the interest rate on many student loans. The NPV of the math major is still positive, but far smaller, about $428K. The film studies major faces a significantly negative NPV—negative $83K.

College can be a good investment, but many college degrees are really consumption, not investment: they do not enhance the student's earning power enough to cover college's costs.

> Do not make important personal decisions based on this toy example. Many elements are simplified:
>
> - Earnings projections for each degree and occupation.
> - A strictly illustrative discount rate.
> - Differences in unemployment rates are omitted (college unemployment rates are one-third that of high school graduates).
> - Changes in earnings over time are omitted for simplicity.
> - Assumes a forty-five-year career, which may be longer or shorter than your actual career.

Nevertheless, **this example does suggest the importance of choosing wisely to assure that your investment in higher education is actually investment and not merely a very expensive consumption item**.

You may have wondered why for most people, college comes in a very specific interval between about ages 17 and 22. You realize that attending higher education earlier would mean omitting some preparation in high school, while going later reduces the number of post-college years in which you can exploit the new knowledge. All true, but expressed more crisply in financial terms: **at these ages the opportunity cost of college is quite low, and the time period over which benefits** (positive cashflows) **will be earned is longest**.

The main purpose of this simplified example is to illustrate NPV calculations in an relatable instance. It also highlights several other important elements of the NPV framework:

1) Often the analysis hinges on the differences in cashflows between the status quo and each option.
2) There is always a baseline trajectory of cashflows, so what is relevant for any option is its differences from that baseline. If the baseline is "do nothing," its cashflows are zero, by definition. But in many instances the baseline is not zero. In the above case, the baseline was going to work with only a high school degree. The effects of college are not the alumnus's entire post-college earnings, but the difference between those earnings and the baseline.
3) The length of time over which the benefits of the investment are enjoyed is critical. If any major resulted in being unemployed say, 10% of the time, the NPV would drop precipitously, because benefits would be at least 10% less but costs would not change. If the alumnus's post-graduate career was less than forty-five years, that would also reduce the NPV. By contrast, extending their career would increase the NPV, but less than proportionately because the last years of the career will be discounted the most.
4) Discount rate matters greatly, especially for a long-lived investment. The math major's NPV at a 6% discount rate is about one fourth than that of a 0% discount rate (i.e., undiscounted). The 6% discount rate is enough to change the sign of the film studies major's NPV from (barely) positive to negative.
5) Clearly, the cashflow projections are the foundation of any NPV analysis. A math major has a superior NPV because his or her projected earnings are far greater than a film studies major. In this toy example those earnings did not change over time. In reality it is likely that the math major's earnings would rise far more rapidly than the film studies major, and the high school graduate's earnings will probably not stay constant, but erode. Introducing more realistic assumptions would magnify the differences in NPVs.

You will find it a very valuable exercise to project cashflows for options you are considering and compute their NPVs at plausible discount rates. This will help you choose among your options. Even more importantly, it may demonstrate that none of your options are attractive enough, if their NPVs are negative or unimpressive.

Uncertainty

In real life, future cashflows aren't entirely certain. For example, if there is a recession, sales will drop and positive cashflows will shrink. NPV calculations can create a false sense of precision.

The way to account for uncertainty is to acknowledge it openly. In essence, ask the "what if?" questions: What if some future condition occurs that is different than my most likely assumptions? Analysts call these alternative assumptions *scenarios*. An analysis is repeated for each scenario to determine how the decision impacts change. This is called *sensitivity analysis*: Is the decision sensitive to the different assumptions?

The superior options are those that will produce acceptable results over a wide range of scenarios. For example, an option that produces a positive but modest NPV in pessimistic scenarios may be preferred to one that produces a bigger positive NPV, but only under optimistic scenarios.

Table 7-3 shows an example sensitivity analysis. In this case we are considering building a $20M apartment building on a vacant lot, which is expected to earn $2.5M per year by renting its apartments. The rents it will earn depend heavily on its vacancy rate—the fraction of apartments that will not be rented. This is driven mainly by economic conditions: a strong economy will attract in-migrants, while a weak economy will prompt local residents to migrate to better conditions elsewhere.

Our baseline economic forecast assumes a "normal" economy that grows at 3% per year, with rents growing similarly. However, in a boom year rents have grown at 6% a year, while in a recession year rents have fallen at 10% per year.

The basic cashflows, shown in the "undiscounted" columns, differ considerably due to assumed economic conditions: the $2.5M annual rental income grows by Year 10 to over $3.25M per year in a boom, but falls to less than $1M a year in a recession. This has a dramatic effect on the NPV, since the construction cost is assumed to be the same in each scenario. The apartment building's return falls short of its $20 M cost--$4.46 M, in fact--even in a boom, but loses far more--$10.55 M--if a recession occurs. In a normal economy its losses fall in between, $6.85 M. Clearly the wisdom of building this apartment building is very sensitive to the economy!

Again, this is a toy example to make the mechanics easy to follow. A real version of this analysis would differ in several ways:

- Abnormal economic conditions do not persist for ten years. A recession might last, say, two or three years. The assumed growth rate in rents probably should vary across the decade-long projection horizon. The actual differences among these economic scenarios would not be so dramatic.
- The apartment building is probably not worth zero—ceases generating rental income—in Year 11, as the table implicitly assumes. Commonly, analysts assume a salvage value or terminal value at the conclusion of the horizon, as we did in figure 6-1. It can be the expected resale value of the asset or the present value of its expected earnings beyond the horizon. These two values should be very similar, as Chapter XV will show.

Table 7-3

Sensitivity analysis: Effects of economic uncertainty on apartment building value							
Percentages shown are rental income growth rates under alternative economic scenarios							
		Undiscounted (FVs)			Discounted (at DR=) 5% (PVs)		
		Recession -10%,	**Normal economy 3%**	**Boom 9%**	**Recession -10%**	**Normal economy 3%**	**Boom 9%**
YEAR							
0		-$20.00	-$20.00	-$20.00	-$20.00	-$20.00	-$20.00
1	5	$2.50	$2.50	$2.50	$2.50	$2.50	$2.50
2	5	$2.25	$2.58	$2.65	$2.04	$2.34	$2.47
3	5	$2.03	$2.65	$2.81	$1.59	$2.08	$2.33
4	5	$1.82	$2.73	$2.98	$1.17	$1.76	$2.09
5	5	$1.64	$2.81	$3.16	$0.83	$1.42	$1.78
6	5	$1.48	$2.90	$3.35	$0.56	$1.09	$1.45
7	5	$1.33	$2.99	$3.55	$0.36	$0.80	$1.12
8	5	$1.20	$3.07	$3.76	$0.22	$0.56	$0.83
9	5	$1.08	$3.17	$3.98	$0.13	$0.37	$0.58
10	5	$0.97	$3.26	$4.22	$0.07	$0.23	$0.39
				NPV	-$10.55	-$6.85	-$4.46
				PV (benefits)	$9.45	$13.15	$15.54
				PV (costs)	-$20.00	-$20.00	-$20.00

- In addition to economic uncertainty, other types of uncertainty might matter:
- Construction overruns might raise the building's cost above $20M, or might delay completion beyond one year.
- Government mandates might require some units to be rented at below-market rates.
- The building manager might find additional ways to earn rental income, such as renting the ground floor to more lucrative retail tenants.

These changed assumptions can be incorporated to create several different scenarios represented by different future cashflow profiles.

Often analysts blend these different sources of uncertainty into combined scenarios. The analyst uses imaginative names like "best case" and "worst case" scenarios. We are not fans of this approach because it hides the specific uncertainty to which the decision is most sensitive. And who is to say that their imagination has really grasped the best case and the worst case?

Conclusion

An investment is worth making only if it really is an investment, not consumption. That means it generates more income than it costs, after accounting for the time value of money. In practice this means discounting all of its cashflows—positive and negative—by a discount rate (DR), adjusted for the amount of time in the future when the cashflow will occur. That DR should be the investor's *opportunity* cost—the best rate of return he or she could earn investing in an alternative of similar riskiness to the investment under consideration. Subtracting the sum of the present value of the investment's costs from the present value of its benefits produces **a net present value (NPV)**. Positive NPV investments are worth undertaking; negative NPV investments aren't.

NPV computations can be greatly affected by:

- The trajectory of the undiscounted benefits cashflows: Will they grow or shrink? Growth enhances NPV; shrinkage degrades it.
- The duration of the benefit period: longer periods help NPV; shorter periods degrade it. In this sense advocates of the payback shortcut have a point: all else equal, the sooner your assets pays back its cost, the better, because the benefit period can always end abruptly due to some surprise.
- The discount rate. Low discount rates favor all investments, but most especially those whose main benefits come well in the future. High discount rates depress NPV severely.

Chapter IX will take up how the choice of these and other assumptions can skew an NPV analysis.

The NPV framework is the most fundamental idea in this book. It is very much in your interest to get a spreadsheet and gain some practice on one or more decisions that are personally significant to you.

VIII. An Alternative to NPV: Internal Rate of Return (IRR)

As noted in the prior chapter, one subtlety of NPV is that the discount rate chosen is crucial. In most normal investments' trajectories—where costs come early and benefits come later—the higher the discount rate, the lower the NPV. **At a high enough DR, NPV can become negative** because the downstream benefits are so heavily discounted they are less than the near-term costs.

This suggests an alternative way to frame the problem:

Not "What is the NPV at a a specified DR?",

but "At what DR does the NPV turn from positive to negative?"

In other words, a*t what DR does the NPV equal zero*? This DR is known as the **internal rate of return, or IRR**.

Table 8-1 shows how NPV behaves at alternative discount rates for the apartment building from the previous chapter, for the "normal economy" scenario. We simply re-ran that NPV multiple times, each time raising the DR by 0.5%.

Table 8-1

How discount rate (DR) affects net present value (NPV)
Apartment building from table 7-3; "Normal economy" scenario; NPVs in $ millions

DR	NPV
0.0%	$5.40
0.5%	$4.75
1.0%	$4.13
1.5%	$3.52
2.0%	$2.94
2.5%	$2.38
3.0%	$1.84
3.5%	$1.32
4.0%	$0.82
4.5%	**$0.34**
5.0%	**-$0.13**
5.5%	-$0.59
6.0%	-$1.02

As expected, NPV declines at higher discount rates, enough so that it becomes negative somewhere between a DR of 4.5% and 5.0% (shown in bold). NPV is zero at a DR of roughly 4.85%. So this project has an IRR of roughly 4.85%.

This is the project's "rate of return." It generates an average of 4.85% annual return, which just counterbalances a 4.85% discount rate.

With a "normal" investment like this one—where cashflows are initially negative, change sign to become positive, then remain positive thereafter—IRR is unambiguous. Some businesses use it as a criterion for evaluating investments: they compare the IRR to the business' cost of capital, often known as a "**hurdle rate**." (As in, a height the project must "hurdle over" to be approved.) This is a natural and intuitive criterion. But it has two problems.

First, there is no algebraic way to compute IRR. Trial and error must be used, trying alternative DRs until one is found where NPV = 0. Even the IRR macros on spreadsheet programs or financial calculators use this approach. It isn't particularly cumbersome, but it takes a bit of time.

Second, not all projects are well-behaved. **If the sign of the cashflows changes more than once**—for example, if a significant sum must be invested in the apartment building in, say, Year 8—**the project can have more than one IRR**. If each of the computed IRRs is greater than the hurdle rate, the project should still be approved. But what if one IRR falls below and one above the hurdle?

To become familiar with IRR, take one of the decisions you have analyzed to learn NPV and re-run it at several discount rates to find the approximate DR where NPV equals zero.

The IRR is your investment's annual rate of return. If it is greater than your cost of capital, the investment adds value--increases the value of your enterprise. If less than your capital cost, it is subtracting value--it is not earning back the capital it consumes.

IX. How to Rig a Study

NPV may be precise, but the assumptions and data underlying it are subject to judgment, and manipulation. This chapter's title, "How to Rig a Study," is tongue in cheek. Its serious purpose is to help you be aware of how your assumptions, or those of analysts whose work you rely on, can bias the analysis.

Symmetry in Treatment of Costs and Benefits

Bias can creep into your analysis if you treat the two types of cashflows—costs and benefits—asymmetrically. Optimists may inflate benefits and omit some costs. Pessimists may include every conceivable cost but dismiss some benefits. It is important to be equally thorough on both sides of the ledger.

Time Horizon

The longer the period you analyze, the higher the NPV is likely to be—under the usual situation where benefits rise continually over time. It is important to project cashflows only for a realistic period. Most real property has a finite life—machines depreciate; equipment obsolesces. Assuming an indefinite lifespan is probably unreasonable, and it certainly skews the NPV analysis in the investment's favor.

One way to keep yourself honest is to compute NPV for several different time horizons: your assumed lifespan, and one or more shorter periods. See how long you must own the investment to assure a positive NPV. Consider the unpredictable factors that might require you to abandon the investment prematurely.

Discount Rate

Table 8-1 shows how the discount rate can profoundly affect an investment's NPV. This is because costs are usually front-loaded (occur early) while benefits are back-loaded. So discounting later cashflows (benefits) more heavily via a higher DR will suppress them but have little effect earlier cashflows (costs).

The correct DR is essential to an unbiased NPV analysis. As we've said, it should be based on the investment's opportunity costs: the rate of return of the best alternative that must be foregone to make this investment. Advocates often play mischief with discount rates to skew their analyses. Proponents choose a low DR, and opponents choose a high DR.

IRR

As noted in chapter VIII, comparing an investment's IRR to a hurdle rate—the firm's cost of capital—is reasonable, so long as the investment has well-behaved cashflows, where positive cashflows follow negative ones in time and the sign of the cashflows changes only once (from negative to positive). Naïve analysts, or unscrupulous advocates, may bias an analysis by comparing the hurdle rate to the wrong IRR if there is more than one (because the sign of cashflows changes more than once.).

Keeping Inflation Straight

Inflation is a general rise in prices, also known as a decline in the purchasing power of money. Cashflows can be stated in either nominal terms, ignoring the effects of inflation, or real terms. Either is possible, but it is important to label clearly which inflation treatment you use. This will also affect your choice of discount rate. Nominal rates of return include the effects of inflation, while real rates remove it. Careless or malicious analysts may be inconsistent.

X. Benefit/Cost Analysis

Those more interested in public policy than business may have heard of policies tested using "cost-benefit analysis," more formally known as benefit/cost analysis.

Although government does not exist to make a profit, officials should still be concerned with choosing the most efficient policy to achieve a given objective. Even more important, they should ensure that the public will receive more benefits from a policy than they must sacrifice in tax revenues. You will not be surprised to know that the same finance framework presented above is used to evaluate public policy.

Benefit/Cost Analysis

In this type of analysis—very common in government—analysts estimate the public benefit of a policy and compare it to the policy's costs. Since these occur at different times, their analysis discounts each. A net present value is the excess of the policy's benefits over its costs. If several alternatives have positive NPV, they can be ranked by NPV or by their benefit/cost ratio, equivalent to the profitability index described in the next chapter.

Cost-Effectiveness Analysis

Benefit/cost analysis requires that both sides of the ratio be expressed in the same units, usually dollars. Although there are a number of ways to "monetize" nonmonetary benefits such as improved health, all are somewhat arbitrary and subject to manipulation. Many decisionmakers are understandably skeptical of such monetizations —how much is a human life really worth?— and prefer to compare alternatives in their natural units. For example, which option saves the most lives per dollar? Framing the question this way avoids the need to place a value on human lives. But this prevents the use of NPV, which requires both benefits and costs to be in the same units (usually money).

Sometimes the choice is simply one of choosing the most efficient option. Cost-effectiveness analysis works in such situations. Analysts determine which alternative achieves the maximum benefit for a fixed budget. Or instead, they fix the level of benefit required, and identifies the alternative that delivers it at the least cost.

I have performed analyses for two sitting US presidents, numerous presidential candidates, and four state governors. In my experience, they are skeptical of monetizing benefits and instead prefer natural units. Cost-effectiveness analysis was much more persuasive.

XI. Multiple Projects: Capital Budgeting

Thus far, our decisions have been binary ones: whether or not to approve a specific project. Real life is far more complex. This chapter will cover one of the most common complexities: allocating a finite amount of capital among several competing projects, when more than one may be simultaneously possible. This is known as *capital budgeting*.

In a corporate setting, this often occurs in annual planning for the following year. Based on the firm's just-closing financial results, the CEO will know how much the firm will have to invest in growth (retained earnings) and how much of that amount will be budgeted for capital expenditures. NPV analyses can be conducted for each candidate project. But what to do if more projects with a positive NPV are available than the capital budget can fund?

At the most basic level, the goal of any firm action—especially investing—is to **increase the value of the firm**. That is what any owner wishes, and what an owner expects of any hired employee, including the firm's senior management. Positive NPV investments add value, which a well-functioning capital market should reflect by raising the firm's stock price.

Theoretically, sensible capital expenditures—that increase the firm's market value—should always occur, without constraint. If a firm has a value-adding investment opportunity, investors should be happy to offer it funds so they can share in the rewards. In practice, though, any number of obstacles can intrude. Market sentiment may currently undervalue the firm's stock, requiring too many shares be sold to meet the capital need. The firm may not wish to take on additional investors and dilute current ownership. Or the firm may have other plans for raising financing later and wish to avoid distracting investors with the current proposals.

A simple and reasonable approach is to rank the projects in terms of their NPV, and invest in projects (beginning with the first ranked, and descending in ranking) until the budget is exhausted. This is an adequate approach, but it can be improved.

NPV Ranking vs. "Bang for the Buck"

The project that will add the most value is the one with the highest NPV. So a simple implementation is to rank projects by NPV and select them in rank order until you exhaust the capital budget. The ranked set should include all positive-NPV projects.

As simple approaches go, this is very good, but not ideal. Say that you have three projects: A, B, and C have similar NPVs, but A costs twice as much as B or C. For example:

	Cost	NPV
Project A:	$20M	$3M
Project B:	$10M	$2.8M
Project C:	$10M	$2.7M

A has a slightly higher NPV, but B's and C's NPVs—almost as good—are each achieved in projects that cost only half as much as A. So B and C each offer much greater "bang" (NPV) for the "buck" (cost).

Profitability

To capture "bang for the buck," we can add the additional criterion of a project's profitability: How much NPV does it generate per dollar of cost? The "profitability index" is simply:

Profitability index = NPV/Cost

The above table is repeated with profitability added.

	Cost	NPV	Profitability index
Project A:	$20M	$3M	0.15
Project B:	$10M	$2.8M	0.28
Project C:	$10M	$2.7M	0.27

Clearly, both projects B and C offer much more bang for the buck than project A. If your budget is $10M, choose B. If it is $20M, choose B and C: that portfolio of projects has a profitability index of 0.275 (or [2.8 + 2.7]/20), almost twice that of A.

A better budgeting rule than simple NPV ranking would be to rank all projects by profitability index. Select those projects in profitability index order until your budget is fully consumed. Omit any projects with negative NPVs, which will also have negative profitability indexes.

XII. When Might a Firm Invest Outside Its Own Projects?

Warren Buffett purchased a failing textile firm, Berkshire Hathaway, and converted it into a holding company for a wide range of operating businesses including Geico, See's Candies, BNSF Railway, and several electric utilities. Berkshire's annual return has been roughly double that of the overall stock market (20% vs. 10%) for *over fifty years*. This historic record has earned Buffett the mantle of greatest living investor. Buffett has a knack for buying whole companies with a dominant competitive advantage in their markets, so their earnings are growing and predictable. But before Berkshire began buying whole companies, Buffett ran an investment partnership that purchased minority stakes (blocks of stock) in publicly traded companies. His ability to select winning stocks, learned at the feet of the father of value investing Ben Graham, is legendary.

Berkshire and its subsidiaries hold a portfolio of publicly traded securities that usually accounts for about half of the firm's total market capitalization. Furthermore, it is often highly concentrated, with more than half composed of only three or four stocks.

Why might a firm that owns entire brand name companies choose also to be a minority shareholder in other firms?

Diversification

Spreading your bets among firms or industries can reduce your risk. A firm typically develops expertise in its industry and naturally concentrates its holdings. That leaves it vulnerable to industry cycles.

An oil company's profits suffer when oil prices are low. By contrast, an airline's profits soar under the same circumstances, because fuel is the single largest cost of airline operation. Owning some stock of firms in each industry can smooth out an individual investor's portfolio returns. It is a small step to viewing the assets of a firm like Berkshire Hathaway the same way. Buffett clearly views Berkshire as a portfolio, as he should.

Liquidity

Even a serial acquirer like Berkshire will not always have attractive acquisitions available. Buffett prefers to buy "when blood is in the streets"—when a company's stock prices are depressed by a temporary corporate crisis or poor general economic conditions. These events are uncommon and hard to predict.

Households maintain an "emergency fund" for (unwanted) surprises. Investors should "keep some powder dry" for unexpected opportunities. Typically, such funds are held in cash, which has the greatest possible liquidity. Certainly some cash is useful, but larger contingency funds, held for longer periods, can earn higher returns in liquid low-risk stocks and stock equivalents. (We will discuss these in Part II.)

For individual investors, financial advisers suggest dividing your total portfolio into multiple "envelopes" or "buckets":

- Envelope 1 contains funds you will spend within one to two years, which should be held in cash or near cash instruments that you need access to quickly.
- Envelope 2 will be spent in three to seven years, held in bonds, dividend-paying stocks, and hybrids such as warrants.
- Envelope 3 is your long-term holdings (e.g., your funds earmarked for retirement), which should be invested for growth.

My book *It's the INCOME, Stupid!* covers this approach to personal financial planning in some detail.

Many corporations take a similar approach, viewing their total balance sheet as a portfolio and segmenting their assets for different purposes and time horizons. For Berkshire, its direct acquisition of entire companies fills its Envelope 3. Minority stock positions compose the bulk of its Envelope 2. (Cash and short-term bonds are Envelope 1.)

Inferior Internal Opportunities

Every dollar of earnings retained and invested should add to the value of the firm. This means that the rate of return for each new investment should exceed the average for all of the firm's existing assets. This average is the firm's *return on equity, or ROE*—simply its profits/stockholders' equity. That is what a *hurdle rate* does; it forces new investments to be discounted at the firm's *cost of capital*: the returns investors demand based on the alternatives available to them. Equity investors will compare Firm A's ROE to the best ROE available in a firm of similar riskiness.

But what if the firm is in a mature industry, and returns available from organic (internal) growth are unimpressive? Diversify. The firm can start slowly, by buying stock positions in other opportunities. As it gains experience, it can later acquire firms in the new industry in whole.

There may be greener pastures (better returns) elsewhere because of differences in basic industry conditions. Or it may be a simple matter of timing. Buying a stock whose price has been temporarily depressed by, say, 50% will double your return when its price rises back to normal. This is the fundamental premise of value investing: investors are irrational, and they overreact to bad and good news. A cool-headed investor who is patient can buy great stocks when others are dumping them. Buffett says, "When others are greedy, be fearful; when they are fearful, be greedy."

As mentioned earlier, Berkshire's long-term return has been about twice the stock market average. That is a high hurdle indeed, with many implications for how Buffett allocates capital. One is that he refuses to pay a dividend; we will take that up in a future chapter. Another is that internal growth opportunities must meet a high standard (hurdle). It would be foolish to ignore the universe of external possibilities—especially once every decade or so (such as 2001 or 2008) when they go on sale.

I Summary of Part I

Deploying Capital

Why Firms Need Capital

(1) New firms have expenses before they have revenue, so startup capital is necessary. In small quantities it can come from "friends, family, and fools" or from the entrepreneur's savings account and credit cards. But as the firm scales up, it will probably need larger infusions of capital. This can come from private investors up to a point, but eventually the magnitude of the need can only be met by drawing upon millions of investors—i.e., from the capital markets. Capital can be equity (partial ownership) or debt (a loan).

(2) The need for capital will recur if the firm wishes to grow, since each new project—a new store or a new product—is a new small business. Firms can finance their growth entirely from past profits (known as "retained earnings"), but then the pace of its growth is limited by those profits. Great opportunities can attract external capital, lured in by their high returns.

Time Value of Money

(3) Money isn't free. An investor who commits his funds to Investment A for a period forecloses using them for Investment B. In other words, money has an opportunity cost. This is generally expressed as an interest rate: opportunity cost per time period.

(4) If, say, I charge you a 10% per year interest rate to rent my money for a year, next year you must repay the $100 you borrow from me plus $10 in interest, or $110. If that is my best investment option, it sets my benchmark for judging other investments.

(5) If I equally prefer $110 a year from now to $100 today, I am implicitly saying that money has a 10% time value for me. To tempt me to part with my money for a year, you need to offer me at least 10% annually.

(6) I will evaluate any investment by "charging" (discounting) it for this time value. So I will discount the future value Investment B offers back to its present value; in this case I will discount future values by 10% per year. If the return is several years in the future, I will discount it for each year.

(7) The formulas are:

a. Future Value (FV) = Present Value (PV) x [1 + Discount Rate (DR)] ^ N (Number of years). This is the standard compounding formula. Rearranging this gets you the present value formula:

b. PV = FV x 1/[1 + DR] ^ N

(8) By converting all future values into a common timescale (the present), they can be added together. Thus the present value of a stream of payments is simply the sum of each payment's present value.

(9) PVs are reduced under either of the following two conditions:

a. A higher DR; or

b. A long time until the payment will come.

(10) Discounting makes equal-sized payments made later worth progressively less in present value terms. Payments far enough in the future will have a PV of essentially zero. Therefore even perpetuities—assets that make payments forever, like equity—do not have an infinite value, because their payments in the far future will have negligible present value.

(11) While computing each payment's PV and adding them together (such as in a spreadsheet) is the best way to learn these calculations, and some shortcuts exist:

a. The Rule of 72 allows you to approximate the time need for an amount to compound to double its original value, or any level that is a factor of 2x original value such as 4 = 2^2, or 8 = 2 ^3.

b) if you know the starting and ending values, the rule of 72 will estimate the annual growth rate between them.

c. The PV of a perpetuity that begins immediately is x 1/DR.

d. The PV of a perpetuity that begins N years in the future is:

(Annual payment) x 1/[(DR x (1 + DR)) ^ N]

e. So the PV of a payment that begins immediately and continues for N years is the difference between the a and b, or:

(Annual payment) x ([1/DR] – [1/(DR x (1+DR)) ^ N])

Comparison of investment valuation methods

Method	How it works	Pitfalls/cautions	Comments
Payback	Years until benefits = costs	Ignores later cashflows	Simple rule of thumb
ROI	Benefits/costs – 1	Ignores time value of money	Simple rule of thumb
NPV	PV (benefits) – PV (costs)	Usually requires a spreadsheet	NPV heavily affected by DR and N
IRR	DR where NPV = 0	Unusual cashflow profiles may have multiple IRRs	Can compare IRR to hurdle rate (cost of capital)
Profitability Index	NPV/PV (costs)	Must first compute NPVs	Assures most profit per $ of investment

The two entries in **bold** are the two methods generally considered superior.

Risk

(12) Riskier assets must offer a higher return to attract investors, so they must offer a risk premium over that of a risk-free investment. The premium is included in a higher discount rate.

(13) Since stockholders are behind bondholders among a firm's creditors, equity investments require a larger risk premium than fixed income investments.

Investment Criterion: Net Present Value (NPV)

(14) Common rules of thumb to evaluate investments include:

a. Payback: how long it takes until positive cashflows (benefits) accumulate to equal negative cashflows (the investment's cost).

b. Return on investment (ROI): the ratio of benefits divided by costs for a specified period.

c. Each of these has value as shortcuts, but both ignore the time value of money, and any benefits (or costs) beyond the time period chosen.

(15) A superior approach—the fundamental, gold standard method of evaluating an investment—is its net present value (NPV). It simply subtracts the present value of an investment's costs from the PV of its benefits. Positive PVs add value; negative PVs subtract value.

(16) NPV can be used for a very wide range of investing decisions, including personal ones like investing in your human capital: the NPV of college.

(17) NPVs are only as good as their underlying cashflow projections. Because they are about the future, they are inherently uncertain. For example, a new factory's returns will depend heavily on the number of units it sells, which is dependent on uncertain economic conditions. Analysts use sensitivity analysis—re-running the same analysis several times under different scenarios—to see the range of NPVs possible.

(18) The choice of discount rate (DR) profoundly affects a project's PV. Benefits that come far in the future are discounted the most. Higher discount rates depress the PV of benefits, sometimes enough to turn a positive PV into a negative one.

(19) Unscrupulous or naïve analysts can skew NPVs by poorly chosen discount rates or time horizons. Project advocates will choose a low DR and very long benefit period, while opponents will do the opposite.

Complement to NPV: Internal Rate of Return (IRR)

(20) Since NPVs can change from positive to negative at high enough DRs, there must be a DR where NPV equals zero. This is the project's internal rate of return (IRR). It is analogous to ROI, but unlike ROI it accounts for the time value of money via discounting.

(21) Another common rule of thumb is to accept all projects with IRRs greater than the company's hurdle rate (usually its cost of capital). This is more intuitive for many nonfinancial types, as it simply compares two rates of return (IRR and hurdle rate).

(22) Like the earlier rules of thumb, IRR isn't bad but can be misleading, because projects with more complicated cashflow patterns can have multiple IRRs. "Complicated" means the cashflows may change sign more than once, such as for a project with significant termination costs like cleanup.

Allocating Among Several Investment Projects: Capital Budgeting

(23) If you have more investment candidates with positive NPVs than you have budget for capital expenditures (capex), you need to choose those that will add the most value. A simple way is to rank the projects by NPV, then select them in order until your budget is exhausted. The problem with this simple approach is that it will favor large projects that are most likely to have the largest NPV.

(24) There may be smaller projects that offer greater "bang for the buck"—NPV per dollar invested. The profitability index captures this. It is simply NPV/cost.

(25) Selecting projects in order of profitability index uses your capex budget most efficiently—it adds the most value per dollar of capex.

(26) Using the profitability index preserves "positive NPV" as your fundamental investment criterion. Any project with a positive profitability index has a positive NPV as a mathematical truism.

Firm Investments in Marketable Securities

(27) Firms may invest outside the firm—commonly in marketable securities such as stock in other firms—for several reasons:

a. Diversification: becoming less dependent on the prospects in their home industry

b. Liquidity: preserving capital for future opportunities

c. Limited organic growth opportunities: mature industries may offer low returns from internal growth

Increasing Shareholder Wealth

(28) Fundamentally, firms exist to provide (and increase) shareholders' wealth. All capital allocation decisions should be made with this goal uppermost. Firms invest capital in projects whose benefits are projected to be of higher present value than their costs—i.e., that have a positive net present value. Budgeting capex for investments—internal or external—that offer the greatest bang for the buck (highest profitability index) keeps faith with shareholders.

Part II

Financing Businesses: Acquiring Capital

XIII. Why Businesses Need Financing

Long after the startup phase is behind them, businesses will continue to need capital. They will need to:

- Recruit and train new employees: no employee generates maximum revenue on his or her first day on the job.
- Replace worn out or obsolete equipment.
- Develop new products to keep up with competitors' innovations.
- Develop new markets, then expand to serve them.

As noted earlier, a company can finance its growth entirely out of retained earnings—profits saved for this purpose. But this greatly restricts the pace of growth. If college students financed their studies entirely out of their past savings they might not be able to complete college until they were well over forty years old.

Companies with the greatest growth prospects need the most financing. Conversely, mature companies that grow only slowly need far less. They may be able to use only a portion of retained earnings and distribute the rest to shareholders as dividends.

The Life Cycle of a Corporation

In its earliest stages a firm may be financed strictly from the savings or personal borrowing of its founder. With luck, these initial funds will get the firm through to product development—say, to the perfection of a prototype.

But much more capital may be needed to commercialize the product. A production facility must be bought or leased, staff must be recruited and trained, the new product must engineered to produce at scale and a sales force must approach buyers, and advertising may need to be bought. All this is expense before any revenue is earned. The expanded scale will require deeper-pocketed investors.

The founders can secure a loan, but that burdens them with a fixed cost (servicing the debt) when revenues may be unpredictable and highly volatile. If their growth prospects are compelling, they can secure capital from venture capitalists (VCs, early-stage investors). Generally the VCs' investment will buy partial ownership of the firm. The estimated valuation for the firm—and therefore the percentage ownership that a given amount of VC investment will get—will be heavily negotiated. Each party (VC and founder) will make an NPV calculation, to establish the firm's value, but their assumptions may be very different.

Years—or rarely, months—later, the firm may have grown enough to need additional capital. If they seek equity, they may wish to issue publicly traded stock: this is known as an initial public offering or IPO. An IPO that lists on a stock exchange provides access to the universe of investors, and tens of trillions in capital.

In the pre-IPO stage, and perhaps for years afterward, the firm may be a growth company. That is, its dominant financial characteristic may be rapid growth. Such growth requires frequent capital infusions. Happily, growth investors seek to own stock in companies with rapidly growing earnings, so additional stock issues may be possible as long as growth remains strong.

Years later, the company will reach a mature stage. Competitors have entered the market and peeled away some of its market share. Technologies or business practices that once were new and provided a major competitive advantage are now widely copied, so that advantage has eroded. Earnings growth has slowed significantly. Firms may no longer need much new capital. In fact, mature firms may begin returning capital to shareholders, either through dividends (recurring scheduled payments) or by buying back shares. Presently the dividends paid amount to about 2% of the value of all shares outstanding. Buybacks shrink the number of outstanding shares, making each share worth more.

Some investors see in dividend payouts or stock buybacks a sign that the firm no longer has good opportunities to reinvest earnings. Apple (AAPL) refrained from paying a dividend for its first thirty-five years. Berkshire Hathaway hasn't paid a dividend in almost fifty years, but it has committed to buy back stock if its price falls below a specified threshold.

Part II will cover how firms finance their activity. The key topic here will be *capital structure*: the mix of debt and equity the firm uses. A related topic will be **payout policy**: Should the firm return capital to shareholders, or retain it? For instance, in Chapter XIII should it pay a dividend (and if so how much), and should it buy back stock (and how much)?

Capital on the Balance Sheet

The purpose of a balance sheet is to provide the information needed to value a firm. The firm's assets—everything it owns—are on the left side, carried at their original purchase price. This *book value* may be a considerable underestimate of some assets' current market value. This is by design under accounting principles, to keep the valuation conservative. Assets are segmented by type and by the speed with which they can be converted to cash.

The right side shows the firm's *liabilities*: all obligations the firm has. These include short-term debt accounts payable—commitments it has made to pay for items received but not yet paid for—and longer-term liabilities such as debts.

The net of assets and liabilities is the firm's *net worth*. It is the basic measurement of the firm's valuation in the market, but its market value rarely is exactly equal to its net worth. Assets are carried conservatively and omit projections of future growth, which are very important to investors. Most of the time, a company's *market capitalization* (its value in the marketplace), which includes its growth prospects, is several times its net worth, or *book value*.

Most of the debt portion of a company's capital structure will show up among liabilities, and all of the equity will be part of net worth.

The next two chapters will take up debt and equity financing in sequence.

XIV. Debt Financing

At their core, debts are loans. They differ only in how they are issued and in the specifics of their terms.

Bonds are the most common debt instruments. Instead of securing a loan from a bank or private parties, a firm may issue a bond. The offering process typically includes one or more investment banks that underwrite the bonds—they commit to purchasing a specific portion of the total issue, usually when they are confident they can resell them to their customers. Very large issues may require a syndicate of several underwriters, organized based on the size of their position.

Each bond has a set of specific features, known as terms. The most common ones are:

- Interest rate (or "coupon"): the fraction of the amount borrowed that the issuer pays each year in recurring interest payments. Bonds once had "coupons" attached that the holder would detach to get interest payments. Physical coupons are rarely used anymore, but the term has stuck. Note that the actual yield on the bond may be considerably different than the coupon rate for reasons outlined later in this chapter.
- Maturity: when the issuer must pay back the principal. Bonds may have very short maturities like three or six months (called "bills" or "notes"), or as long as thirty years ("bonds"). A few bonds have been issued with one-hundred-year maturities; and as mentioned earlier, British consols had indefinite maturities.

In the example shown in figure 7-1, that bond matured in ten years and offered a 5% coupon rate.

Fundamental Idea D: Bond Prices

Bonds are priced in a way that is the mirror image of stocks. The main news that affects the value of a company—and therefore the price of each piece of a company, shares of its stock—are changes in corporate earnings. (Stock prices are taken up in the next chapter.) If earnings fall, the value of the stream of future earnings falls, too, so the discounted PV of the stream declines.

By contrast, the stream of interest payments for a bond is fixed. The dominant news is changes in interest rates. A simplified example will illustrate, but we will take up bond prices in more detail in a few sections.

Say that your $1,000 face value bond is issued with a coupon rate of 5%. That means that from now until the bond matures, you will receive $50 per year in coupon payments, then get your principal back at maturity. If interest rates do not change, your bond's yield will remain at 5%.

But let's assume that interest rates increase, say to 10%. For your bond to remain competitive on the secondary market, it must also offer 10%. But its coupon is 5%. **Instead of the coupon rate changing, the bond's price changes**. In this instance, the price would drop to $500, because the $50 coupon is 10% of $500. Ouch.

This will also be true in reverse: If rates drop to 2.5%, the bond's price will rise to $2,000, because $50 is 2.5% of $2,000. Yay!

All of the above flows directly from the time value of money. In table 7-1 the value of that bond—the PV of the stream of future benefit payments—varied inversely with the discount rate: $100 at 5% and $11.56 at 50%. That interest rate can change for two basic reasons:

a) The issuer's riskiness changes, so investors demand a higher or lower discount rate.

b) The market interest rate changes, so the bond's coupon rate becomes more or less competitive.

Bonds are viewed as the sleepy neighborhood of Wall Street, but this isn't entirely justified. As we will see, if you buy a bond and hold it until maturity, you can predict exactly what your return will be. But because the bond's price can change significantly, its value—on paper at least—can be quite volatile.

Bond prices are quoted as a percentage of par value, or 100%. So a bond whose price is quoted as 90 is selling at a 10% discount to par. A price of 120 is a 20% premium to par.

Coupon vs. Yield to Maturity (YTM)

If a bond's price can be different from its face value, this means that its true yield—the effective interest rate it pays—can be different from its coupon yield. If you buy a bond for half of par value (i.e., 50), that greatly increases its effective yield if you hold it until maturity.

To explain this, if you buy a bond at 50 and sell it a year later for 60 (say, because interest rates have fallen in the meantime) your return includes the annual interest payment, plus a capital gain due to the increase in the bond's price. (Of course, if rates rose, your bond's price might fall from 50 to 40, generating a capital loss.) This change in the bond's price is only on paper until you sell the bond. (The same is true for a share of stock: you only realize the capital gain or loss when you sell your share.) If you hold the bond until maturity, you are assured of the bond's price: 100, par value. So although a bond's coupons are quoted, a more meaningful way to quote yield is **yield to maturity**, or YTM.

Say a three-year bond with a 4% coupon is selling for 50. Its present value is therefore $50, based on three years of discounted cashflows. The basic formula is (as before):

PV =[$4/(1 + Y)^1] + [$4/(1 + Y)^2] + [$104/(1 + Y)^3]

where we use Y instead of DR to underscore that we are valuing a bond. Each cashflow is $4 because that is the coupon payment on a $100 face value (par value) bond. The Year 3 cashflow is $104 because it includes both the coupon payment and the repayment of principal.

To compute the bond's yield to maturity, we remember that the market has already established that its PV is $50. So the valuation equation becomes:

$50 = [$4/(1 + Y)^1] + [$4/(1 + Y)^2] + [$104/(1 + Y)^3]

We need to solve for Y to determine the YTM. This can't really be done other than by trial and error. Table 14-1 shows the bond's value for several alternative yields.

Table 14-1

Three-year bond, 4% coupon: Bond values under several alternative YTMs							
		YTM					
YEAR	Cashflow	4%	10%	20%	30%	32%	40%
1	4	3.84615	3.63636	3.33333	3.07692	**3.03030**	2.85714
2	4	3.69822	3.30579	2.77778	2.36686	**2.29568**	2.04082
3	4	3.55599	3.00526	2.31481	1.82066	**1.73915**	1.45773
3	**100**	88.89964	75.13148	57.87037	45.51661	**43.47887**	36.44315
	TOTAL PV	100	85.07889	66.29630	52.78107	**50.54401**	42.79883

Note: Year 3 interest and principal payments shown separately.

In this case the bond's YTM is roughly 32%, because it is necessary to discount all of its cashflows by that rate to produce a present value equal to its current market price of $50. So if you bought this bond at $50 and held it until it matured three years later, your annual return would be 32%. That is the YTM for a bond priced at $50 that generates $4 in annual interest payments plus $100 in principal in Year 3. Notwithstanding their staid reputation, bonds can earn high returns if bought at a large enough discount. (But do not expect such great discounts very often, except when they are accompanied by great risk.)

Bond prices and interest rates therefore move in opposite directions: higher rates depress bond prices, and lower rates raise prices. But the extent of the swings in price due to interest rate changes depends on the bond's maturity, as will be explained shortly. For example, if rates rose from 32% to 40% the price of the bond in table 14-1 above would drop from $50.54 to $42.80.

Yield-to-Call and Yield-to-Worst

Some bonds have call provisions. This means that if interest rates drop, the issuer can repay the bond--call it in--in order to issue new bonds at the new, lower rate. Typically call provisions specify that the bond cannot be called any sooner than, say, ten years after issuance. An early redemption of the bond will lower its yield. so many bonds are quoted for a worst-case scenario, where the bond matures early due to its being called. Quotes may indicate not only a YTM, but a "yield to call" or "yield to worst"; that is the lowest yield the bond may provide.

The Yield Curve

Bonds of longer maturities generally must offer a higher YTM. The reason is risk.

Investors are compensated for each year of opportunity costs via coupon payments, with the YTM reflecting their discount rate. Longer-term bonds are exposed to more years (greater risk) of surprises. A ten-year bond is exposed to possible negative events for ten years; a thirty-year bond is exposed for three times as long. Not surprisingly, YTMs are higher for bonds of longer maturities. The graph of this relationship is known as the yield curve. It isn't unusual for thirty-year bonds to have YTMs 3: i.e., 3% or 4% (i.e., 300 to 400 basis points, or bps) higher than very short-term bonds from the same issuer.

Exposure to Interest Rate Swings: Duration

The price of a long-term bond is inherently more subject to change than that of a short-term bond. If interest rates rise by a point (1%) , i.e. within parenthesis: "or 100 basis points", a three-year bond's coupon is only offering a below-market payment for three years. By contrast, the owner of a thirty-year bond is stuck with three decades of below-market payments.

Duration is a measure of the midpoint in the expected cashflows an investor will receive from a bond. Specifically, it is the average of the times of all of its cashflows, weighted by the size of the cashflow. In table 14-1, at 4% YTM, duration would be computed as follows, where PVi is the discounted cashflow for year i:

$$\text{Duration} = (\text{PV1} \times 1 + \text{PV2} \times 2 + \text{PV3} \times 3)/\text{Total PV, or}$$
$$(3.85\text{x}1 + 3.70\text{x}2 + 92.46\text{x}3)/100 = 2.89 \text{ years}$$

So the bond buyer will not see the present value of half of the bond's positive cashflows (i.e., half its total value) returned to him until about the tenth month of the third year.

The midpoint of cashflows typically comes well after the midpoint of the maturity schedule, as in the example above, because repayment of principal is a very large cashflow which does not occur until maturity.

Duration is not simply a scheduling exercise. You may read in the financial press that, for example, a bond with a duration of five years will experience price swings five times the magnitude of a swing in interest rates. In this case, when interest rates drop by 1%, a bond with a duration of five years would see a 5% price increase. The press is actually using language somewhat loosely: strictly speaking, this relationship is known as modified duration. It is sometimes called volatility. Volatility is computed as:

Volatility (modified duration) = Duration / 1 + YTM

For a fairly small YTM, this can be approximated as volatility = duration/1, which is how the press interprets it. Although the correct term is modified duration or volatility, this is often simply called duration.

The greater volatility of longer-term bonds should make intuitive sense, once you remember that a long-term bond will pay its owner a stream of cashflows for many years. If their coupon rate deviates from market rates (because rates have changed since the bond was issued), the owner will enjoy a windfall if rates have fallen, and suffer paper loss if rates have risen. Remember, though, that the bond's price will always converge to par value at maturity, because that is the amount the bondholder will receive in principal repayment.

Other Types of Bonds

Wall Street is endlessly inventive in developing new financial products to respond to apparent investor demand. So while the standard fixed income bond described above is by far the most prevalent, other types have blossomed in response to perceived need. This section will briefly describe several types.

Zero Coupons

A standard bond has a duration shorter than its maturity because it pays coupon payments along the way to principal repayment at maturity. This is well suited to investors who wish some income until they are repaid. But what about long-term investors who don't need income in the interim, who can simply park their money and hope to receive a much larger sum at maturity? This is what zero coupons do.

Zeros are so-called because they have no coupon payments. The investor gets no cashflow until their principal is repaid. As a result, zeros sell at a heavy discount, since their entire positive cashflow is well in the future and therefore heavily discounted. The stock analogue to a zero is a growth stock that pays no dividend. Investors' entire return will come from capital gains.

Strips

If a bond can be issued with no coupon payments, the mirror image is also possible: no principal repayment. Originally these two types were created by unbundling traditional Treasury bonds, separating their coupon and principal payments into separate income streams. The stock equivalent would be the (rare) company that pays out dividends on an asset that will eventually become worthless, such as a mine, an oil field, or a patent.

Valuing Zeros and Strips

As you can imagine, both types of bonds sell at sizable discounts. We can unbundle the three-year bond whose cashflows were detailed in table 14-1 to illustrate that discount. Table 14-2 repeats the earlier table, with one small addition: we have separated the third year coupon payment and principal payment into two separate cashflows.

Table 14-2

Earlier bond cashflows separated between interest (strips) and principal (zero coupon)							
		YTM					
YEAR	Cashflow	4%	10%	20%	30%	32%	40%
1	4	3.84615	3.63636	3.33333	3.07692	3.03030	2.85714
2	4	3.69822	3.30579	2.77778	2.36686	2.29568	2.04082
3	4	3.55599	3.00526	2.31481	1.82066	1.73915	1.45773
3	**100**	88.89964	75.13148	57.87037	45.51661	**43.47887**	36.44315
	TOTAL PV	100	85.07889	66.29630	52.78107	50.54401	42.79883
PV interest (strip)		**11.10036**	**9.94741**	**8.42593**	**7.26445**	**7.06514**	**6.35569**
PV principal (zero coupon)		**88.89964**	**75.13148**	**57.87037**	**45.51661**	**43.47887**	**36.44315**

Focusing on the column associated with a 32% yield to maturity (discount rate), the entries for years 1 through 3 in italics show the present value of each coupon payment. These are summed in the footer of the table in italics, showing the present value of all three coupon payments combined: $7.07. That is the present value of $4 in annual payments for three years. This is the value of a strip of this bond. The bold cell shows the present value of $100 principal payment made in the third year: $43.48 in the 32% YTM column. That is the value of a zero coupon version of this bond. Together they of course add up to $50.54, the value of the traditional version of this bond.

Variable Rate Bonds

Bonds are mainly directed to investors who seek a very predictable return, but a few bonds offer a variable rate of return. These types grow in appeal when inflation accelerates, because inflation generally pushes up interest rates. As we've seen, rising rates devastate bond prices, especially for long maturities. So not surprisingly the most common variable rate bonds are those indexed to inflation. Treasury inflation protected securities, or TIPS, offer the largest market of bonds of this type.

TIPS resemble traditional bonds in that they offer a fixed coupon payment. This is designed to elicit interest from traditional bond investors by offering predictable nominal interest payments. The inflation adjustment is made to the principal repayment. If inflation averages, say, 2%, at maturity the principal is repaid at par x (1.02)^N. Bidders at auctions for newly issued TIPS bid on the inflation premium. Economists use this as an indicator of inflation expectations.

Junk Bonds

Formally known as high yield bonds, these are bonds rated below investment grade—below BBB in the S&P and Fitch ratings schemes, often termed "speculative grade." Often the issuers have sketchy prospects or have pledged as collateral assets of uncertain value. Naturally, these require a high risk premium. In the 1980s some investors—most famously Michael Milken of Drexel Lambert—determined that the market risk premiums were excessive: the risk premium was several percentage points higher than the difference (spread) between junk bond default rates and investment grade defaults. Common junk bond spreads over investment grade bonds are 4 to 6%, even though the difference in default rates was less than half as much. However, spreads can widen significantly in bad economic times when many issuers default.

Mortgage-Backed Bonds

A bank that has issued a mortgage to a homeowner holds a long-term stream of cashflows. In the early 1980s Lewis Ranieri of Salomon Brothers realized that many mortgages could be bundled together and securitized—sold to investors. Thus the mortgage backed security (MBS) was born. (This story is colorfully told in Michael Lewis' hilarious *Liar's Poker*.)

MBS provided a valuable service to the banking system, allowing banks to sell off mortgage loans to regain capital that could again be lent out. But every innovation has a price. In the case of MBSs, once banks were no longer dependent on the repayment of their mortgagees, lending standards eroded. This trend was accelerated in the early 2000s when the Federal Reserve expanded the supply of money that banks could lend. Mortgage money chased ever-riskier borrowers, and the *subprime* MBS was born.

Subprime MBSs are similar to long-term junk bonds: they require a high risk premium. In the mad chase for borrowers in the early and mid-2000s, risk premiums vanished. Lenders persuaded themselves that mortgagee's homes were about the safest assets around. No one would voluntarily default on mortgage payments and let their house go into foreclosure (where the lender seizes the collateral in lieu of missed payments), because "house prices always rise." Further, those presumed price increases would permit a borrower at risk of defaulting to roll over (refinance) their mortgage.

In 2006–2007 the merry-go-round came to a stop. House prices, which had not fallen nationwide in seventy-five years, dropped by about 25% nationally, and by as much as 60% in some markets. By late 2007 this crash brought on a general economic recession, with about five million jobs lost. Many of the newly unemployed could no longer make mortgage payments. MBS risk premiums exploded upward, and their prices crashed. The story of a handful of farsighted investors who made money off this trend is told in Michael Lewis' The Big Short, made into a popular movie in 2014. (Shorting is the act of betting that an asset's price will go down.)

Each of the above types of bonds has specific differences from the others, but all can be valued using the framework described in this chapter.

How Bonds Generate Capital for the Issuer

If, say, IBM wishes to raise capital in the debt (bond) market, it will engage an investment bank. That bank will *underwrite* the bond: it will commit to buying a certain proportion of the new issue, usually because it is confident it can resell most or all of this amount to its customers. Investment banks (I-banks) earn an underwriting fee and may charge a commission for resale of their bonds. If an issue is very large, several I-banks may form a syndicate and divide up the new issue. The coupon payment is determined based on the issuers' and their I-bank's sense of what will be most popular among the bond's target market. Any bonds not purchased by the syndicate will be sold at auction, with the final auction price setting the YTM for the bond at issue. Thereafter the bond's price and YTM varies through daily transactions in the market, just as for stocks: more demand will increase prices and lower YTMs, while slack demand will depress prices and raise YTMs.

When the bonds are sold, their proceeds are entered onto the issuer's balance sheet as an addition to assets through the company's paid in capital, and addition to liabilities in its debt. If you buy a bond through your broker, you almost certainly are not buying a new issue. Rather, you are buying in the secondary market, buying from a previous buyer. The issuer got their capital in the initial issue; further transactions are trades among third parties.

The Cost of Debt

All capital has a cost, because all investors require compensation for their opportunity costs. Debt's cost is straightforward: the interest rate being charged—usually the YTM.

There is, however, a more subtle cost, which will be taken up in a later chapter. Debt service becomes part of the firm's fixed costs. Making debt payments doesn't go away when sales slump (unless the firm defaults—stops making debt payments entirely). Therefore undertaking debt commits a firm to siphoning off some of the firm's revenues to a fixed cost. Like any fixed cost, this can pose problems when revenues dip. We will discuss the costs of financial distress in Chapter XVI.

XV. Equity Financing

Shareholders are the mirror image of debtholders. They are entitled to no assured payments; even dividends can be suspended by a firm's board of directors. They are near the back of the line in repayment priority if the firm's assets are liquidated. Common stock, also known as equity because of its place on the balance sheet, is therefore riskier than bonds, and it commands a risk premium.

In exchange, shareholders enjoy all of the upside if the firm grows. Debtholders' payments do not change when the indebted firm prospers —prospers: bondholders are entitled to only interest payments, plus principal repayment at maturity. Shareholders, by contrast, are partial owners of the firm and enjoy proportional shares of all of its (hopefully) rising earnings.

Stock Valuation Uses the Same Framework as Bond Valuation

Any asset's value is the present value of all of its future cashflows. This is an asset's **intrinsic value**—what buyers "should" be willing to pay for it. At any given moment the asset's price may be quite different, for reasons discussed later. So it should be no surprise that the basic framework we developed for bonds can be used to value an equity—a whole company, or a share of its stock.

A bond's cashflows come in two basic types:

- Annual coupon payments, originally expressed as an interest rate (a percentage of the bond's par value)
- Repayment of principal at the maturity of the bond (the scheduled termination of the bond contract)

An equity investment has two analogous cashflows:

- Quarterly dividend payments
- A terminal price for the company/share at the end of a holding period

So the framework and formulas from the previous chapter will serve quite well for equity valuation. There are four main differences, all conceptually minor:

1) Equities labor under a higher risk premium than debt, so the DR will be higher.
2) The company may not issue dividends, so there may be no interim cashflows before the terminal value.
3) Bond earnings (coupon payments) are fixed. Company earnings, and therefore dividends paid to shareholders, hopefully grow.
4) If earnings grow, the terminal value of the company will be greater than its original purchase price.

While the math is straightforward and familiar, the assumptions are open to disagreement. As we have seen, a minor difference in the discount rate can produce big differences in valuation (present value). The same is true for difference in expected terminal value and earnings growth. Investors are hardly unanimous in their judgments about these for any individual company, much less for all equities (the stock market). Further, investing is driven by emotion—greed and fear—as much as by dispassionate analysis, as we will discuss.

Investors who emphasize (2) through (4) are selecting their companies for expected earnings growth; this is often called *growth investing*. They do not expect dividends—in fact, they prefer companies that do not pay dividends when they believe those resources can earn a higher return if reinvested internally. Growth investors' goal is capital gains—a terminal value that is much higher than their purchase price, due to rapid earnings growth. *Income* investors emphasize dividends, so they focus on companies in mature industries with modest capital needs that can afford to pay out much of their earnings to shareholders. *Value* investors are often confused with income investors, but they generally focus on companies whose value other investors are underestimating, often due to the manic depressiveness that frequently grips markets.

Corporate vs. Per-Share Valuation

In this chapter we will generally discuss valuing a share of common stock, but realize this is simply a portion of the entire company. Many equity analysts value companies, then divide that corporate valuation by the number of shares outstanding to value an individual share. Since your first use of these techniques is likely to be for small-scale investments, we will emphasize valuing shares. But recognize that converting shares valuations to company valuations, or vice versa, is a simple matter of multiplication or division.

Equity on a Firm's Balance Sheet

The final item on a balance sheet is *stockholders' equity*, also known as the firm's *net worth*. It is the difference between the firm's left-hand-side assets and right-hand-side liabilities. Since assets are carried at their original cost minus depreciation, equity is often known as *book value*: the value of the firm as carried on its books. As indicated earlier, book value is usually a very conservative representation of a firm's true value, by design.

The Process of Issuing Equity

If you have ever watched an episode of *Shark Tank*, you have seen one way equity is issued: venture capitalists offer capital to a startup in exchange for a piece of the business. This is an example of a *private placement*.

Under current regulations a privately owned firm may have no more than five hundred shareholders; after that, it must "go public." Facebook reached this point in 2012 and reluctantly issued public stock. That process is known as an *initial public offering*, or IPO. The firm seeking investors usually contracts with an investment bank (I-bank) to underwrite the floated stock; that is, they agree to buy a specified block of shares. Typically the I-bank's intent is to re-sell its shares to its customers. The firm is valued (using methods like those described in this chapter), and the number of shares to be issued is decided based on the type of investor being targeted. If retail investors are an important target market, a firm's valuation will be divided into many shares outstanding so that each share is an affordable price for a small investor.

IPOs are promoted with massive "road shows" in which the issuer and its I-banks make pitches about the firm's bright prospects to argue that its IPO shares are probably underpriced. Indeed, the I-bank commonly moderately underprices the shares to assure an immediate "pop" upward of prices in the early days when it is first traded on a stock exchange. Research has shown, however, that such pops are quite short-lived, usually disappearing within days.

As with bonds, after the initial offering, any subsequent trading of the new shares is in the secondary market: even if share prices increase, those gains go to the owners of the shares, not to the issuing firm.

Valuing a Stock: The Dividend Discount Model

We start with the simplest case. Say your company is a utility with a single power plant that you expect to decommission in ten years. In other words, the firm will cease to exist ten years from now. You will only attract income investors, so your firm pays out all of its earnings in dividends (since there is no need to retain earnings for growth you are not planning for). An investor's cashflow stream, then, is simply the stream of ten years of dividends.

Assume the utility will pay a $5 dividend each year for ten years, then nothing thereafter. (For simplicity, assume that there are no net costs or gains from shutting down the power plant: it neither has shutdown costs nor does it have salvage value, or the two net to zero.) The cashflow (future values) trajectory for a share therefore is:

	+$5	$5	$5	$5	$5	$5	$5	$5	$5	$5	$5	$0
YEAR	0	1	2	3	4	5	6	7	8	9	10	11 and thereafter

This is exactly analogous to a strip bond. The value of a share is the present value of the discounted stream of dividends. That value is computed with the **dividend discount model**.

A spreadsheet would allow us to compute this PV by brute force, but as a refresher, let's use the finite annuity shortcut described in chapter IV. The PV of a finite stream of payments over N years is the difference between the PV of a perpetuity and the PV of a perpetuity that begins N years in the future:

PV = Payment x [1/DR – (1 /[DR x (1+DR)^N])]

Let's assume the board pays out a $5 dividend each year. (Dividends are typically paid quarterly, but we will ignore this for now.) Since this is a stable, predictable payment stream, let's assume a 5% discount rate (DR). So in this example the stock's intrinsic value is:

PV (utility stock) = $5 x [1/.05 – (1 /[.05 x (1+.05)^10])], or $38.61

A value investor would argue that if the market price for the stock is, say, $32.00, it is underpriced. Maybe so, but bear in mind that a simple change in the DR from 5% to 7.5% —say, because the company suddenly looks riskier—lowers the stock's value to $31.89. To be successful, value investors have to be confident they are smarter than the market.

The above example uses the finite annuity shortcut. But it is easy to make mistakes with this formula. Personally, I prefer to do it by brute force on a spreadsheet. Each cell's computation can be kept quite simple (i.e., complex chains of formulas can be subdivided among cells). And reviewing patterns in the cashflows quickly points out errors in my keystrokes.

The present value of a stream of constant dividends paid indefinitely is of course a perpetuity: PV = Dividend/DR. At a 5% discount rate, a $5 dividend paid forever would be worth:

PV = $5/.05 = $100.

Put another way, the dividends paid in Years 11 to infinity are worth $61.39 (or $100 – $38.61).

In general, **the value of a share of stock is the sum of the present values of all future payments shareholders will receive**. Heretofore we have included only dividends, but the next section will add other payments such as capital gains. This broader approach is often known as the **discounted cashflow or DCF model**.

More Realism: Adding Horizon/Terminal Value

In the prior example, the firm had zero value after ten years. But in reality, most firms are intended to be "going concerns" indefinitely. So we can make the example more realistic by adding a projected terminal value for the firm at the end of the cashflow period. (This value is sometimes called the horizon value, since it occurs at the end of our cashflow projection horizon.) In our utility example, the firm's management might plan to sell the entire firm after ten years, or merely sell its assets (the power plant). Let's say the projected value of the firm when sold in

Year 10 was $10 million. Distributed over 1 million shares, this would mean each shareholder's proportional entitlement to the "terminal value" is $10. The cashflow profile would now look as follows:

	$5	$5	$5	$5	$5	$5	$5	$5	$5	$15
YEAR	1	2	3	4	5	6	7	8	9	10

The terminal value is exactly analogous to a zero coupon bond. **So the combination of dividends** (like strips) **and terminal value** (like zeros) **gives us a cashflow structure like a traditional bond**. At a 5% discount rate, the extra $10 in value in Year 10 increases the stock's value from $36.81 to $42.38. Put another way, the $10 in terminal value only added $5.57 to the value of the stock, because the added value is discounted for ten years.

Terminal value can stem from a variety of estimates:

- Comparables. Asset prices can be estimated based on actual sale prices for similar assets. Realtors commonly "pull comps" (research comparables) to determine the asking price for their client's home.
- Historical growth rates. As the usual disclaimer says, past performance doesn't guarantee future results, but it's a good place to start. Long-term growth in stock prices has been between 7 and 10% annually.
- Present value of cashflows past the end date. The above examples assumed that our firm closed down, or sold out, after ten years. This doesn't apply to most firms, which expect an indefinite lifespan. But the terminal value approach is still relevant. That value in, say, Year 10 is simply the present value of all of its future earnings, thereafter in perpetuity.

More Realism: Rising Earnings

Estimating the intrinsic value of equity departs from that of bonds in one respect: bonds cannot grow their earnings, but stocks can. (The uncertainty around earnings growth is one of the key drivers of stocks' higher risk premium.)

A simple rule of thumb for estimating the value of a stream of growing dividends adjusts the DR for expected annual earnings growth, G:

PV = Dividend / (DR – G)

You can see that higher earnings growth reduces the denominator and thus raises the value of the stock. Mathematically this formula only makes sense if the dividend growth rate, G, is less than the discount rate, DR.

This model also omits any terminal/horizon value. But it can be added to create:

PV = Dividend / (DR – G) + Horizon value / (1 +DR)^N

Over longer horizons, the terminal/horizon value assumes diminishing importance and the stream of dividends dominates. If your projections are for far into the future, your attention should emphasize dividends, not terminal value (often called "target price" by Wall Street).

Multistage Growth

Uniform dividend growth is a nice simplifying assumption, but it's highly unlikely over any earnings or long period. Companies with competitive advantages that are able to grow quickly for a while find their rivals have copy them and erode their advantage, and their growth rate. More realistic valuations divide the forecast horizon up into several segments with different growth assumptions (usually assuming deceleration). This can be done by computing each dividend's present value on a spreadsheet—my preferred method for reasons mentioned earlier—or by a series of finite annuities, each with its own uniform growth rate.

Payout Policy

Because dividends are so important to estimating intrinsic value, a word on dividend policy is in order.

Firms can choose to reward their shareholders at two times:

- Now, by returning some corporate earnings back to shareholders. This can be done in chunks, by buying stock back from shareholders which supports the market price by introducing a new large buyer; and by reducing the outstanding share count, which makes each remaining share more valuable because it owns a larger proportion of the firm. Instead, the firm can pay shareholders in a stream of quarterly dividends.
- Later, through capital gains. If the firm can earn high returns it will maximize its value by retaining all its earnings and reinvesting them for growth. Buffett's record at the helm of Berkshire Hathaway suggests his decision to foreswear paying dividends has been good for his shareholders, since they would be unlikely to earn as much investing their dividends elsewhere as they can having their "dividends" reinvested into Berkshire.

The portion of earnings distributed to shareholders as dividends is known as the **payout rate**. One minus this ratio (1-payout rate) is the portion the firm keeps as retained earnings, known as the **plowback rate**.

Firms with bright growth prospects typically retain all of their earnings (i.e., their payout ratio is zero and their plowback ratio is 100%). Conversely, mature firms with modest growth potential may choose to pay out a large share of earnings. There is a class of firms (REITs, BDCs, MLPs, and other "pass-through entities," described below) that are exempt from corporate income tax if they pay out at least 90% of their earnings each year. These firms must constantly raise new capital or accept very modest growth rates.

A company's board of directors determines the dividend amount to be distributed each quarter, usually specified on a per-share basis and announced to the business press. Suspending or reducing the dividend is deeply embarrassing and may cause investors to flee the stock, so most companies aim to distribute dividends predictably and stably—if possible, growing the dividend modestly each year.

Stocks are sometimes evaluated in terms their dividend yield: their annual dividend per share divided by the current stock price. A century ago dividend yields were roughly 5%; today they average barely 2%. In general investors are more interested in capital gains than dividends. However, in the next few decades I expect this to change as economic growth in developed nations stays modest, and Baby Boomers become more dependent on dividend income in retirement. My book *Your Macroeconomic Edge* covers this at length, with tips for investors about promising asset classes.

In the meantime, dividends are the ignored stepchildren of stock markets. In many industries—especially technology—initiating a dividend is interpreted as a signal that your fast-growth days are behind you.

For slower-growing companies, investors would be wise to set an upper limit on the acceptable payout ratio of the firms they invest in. Firms need to retain considerable earnings, or they cease growing. Experts suggest dividends aren't sustainable if payout ratios are higher than 50 to 70%.

As an investor, I look for companies that are highly capital efficient—that do not need to reinvest much of their earnings to maintain growth. These firms may use their earnings to diversify, buy back stock, or pay dividends. I disagree with Buffett insofar that Berkshire's decision to eschew a dividend denies me a choice. If it did pay one, I could always use my dividends to buy more Berkshire shares. For many years Buffett had the tax code on his side: dividends were taxed more heavily than capital gains—but that changed with tax reform in the early 2000s.

Valuing a Company

As mentioned earlier, most analysts value entire companies. That is a good way to remind yourself you are valuing a business, not a poker chip (or abstract piece of paper). Converting a company valuation to an individual share simply requires dividing the total valuation by the number of shares outstanding.

Hybrid Equities

Bonds and common stocks are points on the spectrum of risk and return. There are many other asset classes. This section briefly mentions hybrids that fall between bonds and stocks. This list starts with those closest to fixed income assets and progresses to those closest to true equities. The order of the list is somewhat subjective.

Preferred Stocks

Preferred stocks are stocks that pay a coupon payment, called a **dividend**. They are "preferred" because they take precedence over common stocks in any corporate liquidation (that's why those are called "common"), as well as in any payment to the firm's owners. Preferred dividends must be paid before common dividends, but debt payments take precedence over both.

Preferred stocks' hybrid nature is especially visible for convertible preferred. For these, the owner has the right to convert his or her preferred shares into common at a prearranged price, before a pre-established deadline. If the common stock price rises above that level, the preferred owner will receive a windfall by converting to common stocks that are now worth more than their guaranteed conversion price.

Warrants

Warrants are options to purchase common at a prearranged price. When Berkshire was making crisis investments in several floundering companies in 2008 (including GE, Goldman Sachs, and Bank of America), in addition to buying blocks of shares at depressed prices, he negotiated warrants that allowed Berkshire to buy more shares at specified prices. When the stock market recovered, those prices were well below market, offering Berkshire hundreds of millions in capital gains.

Pass-Through Entities (REITs, BDCs, MLPs)

Certain industries enjoy favorable tax treatment. The real estate and construction industries are the best known: the tax subsidy offered to homeowners from the mortgage interest deduction boosts home sales enormously. Since 1960 firms that manage portfolios of real estate have been able to exempt themselves for corporate taxes by incorporating as real estate investment trusts (REITs). REITs own and manage portfolios of properties, collecting rent from tenants. Investors purchase shares on stock exchanges if the REIT is publicly traded, or via private placement. There is a wide range of property types in REITs, include residential single-family homes, multifamily homes, office buildings, retail space, health care facilities, and even self-storage facilities.

Tax considerations affect REITs' attractiveness and their downsides. To be corporate tax exempt, REITs must pay at least 90% of earnings to shareholders in dividends. (Shareholders still pay taxes, at their personal tax rate.) In addition, REIT dividends do not enjoy the favorable lower personal tax rate of "qualified" dividends.

Nevertheless, REITs are popular with income-oriented investors, especially at present when fixed income (bond) interest rates are suppressed by the Federal Reserve.

The success of REITs in attracting investors eventually encouraged other industries to get in on the act. The other major types of pass-through entities are:

- Master limited partnerships (MLPs): These were originally intended to provide capital for energy exploration, but over time MLPs have been created to own energy transmission (pipelines), storage, and other types of infrastructure.
- Business development corporations (BDCs): BDCs make loans to small and midsized companies that are often too risky for traditional banks. BDCs extract a hefty risk premium, though. Most BDC loans are at (high) floating rates, so the lender avoids inflation risk. Many BDCs negotiate "equity kickers": in addition to loan payments, the BDC receives some equity in the borrowing company. Some BDCs receive as much as 15 to 20% of their revenues from managing their equity portfolios.

Pass-through entities are attractive candidates for certain investing goals. More about them is available in my *Your Macroeconomic Edge* and *It's the INCOME, Stupid!*

Conclusion

Valuing equity uses the same framework as valuing debt (bonds). A stock's intrinsic value is the present value of all of its future earnings. This is known as a discounted cashflow, or DCF, approach. The dominant cashflow is dividends, and a secondary cashflow is the terminal or horizon value of the stock at the end of the forecasting horizon. Dividends and terminal value are analogous to coupon payments and principal repayment for a bond.

If dividends are expected to grow, the PV formula is modified to reduce the discount rate by the dividend growth rate. This is only mathematically sensible if the former is larger than the latter.

Firms set a payout ratio that determines the share of earnings paid out as dividends. Some types of firms, known as pass-through entities, are exempt from corporate taxes if they keep their payout ratio at 90% or higher. Although they have limitations, these types of investments will become increasingly popular in the future.

XVI. Fundamental Idea E: Capital Structure: The Debt/Equity Mix

Firms have a choice about how they finance themselves: debt vs. equity. The choice isn't a binary one: firms choose a capital structure that is the mix of the two financing methods that is best for their life cycle stage, capital efficiency, growth needs, and investor goals.

Put yourself in the place of a founder of a startup firm who needs capital. This very risky venture is your best chance to get rich. You can raise equity capital by agreeing with investors on a valuation for the firm and allocating percentage ownership based on their capital infusions. If the firm is valued at $1 million, each $100,000 investment would be entitled to 10% of the shares. To maintain control, you cannot sell more than 49% unless you are confident some of those shareholders will vote your way. Venture capitalists and similar early-stage investors may invest with you, but you can expect to negotiate the firm's valuation. You know by now that many of the assumptions behind an NPV analysis are open to dispute, which can change the valuation by a significant multiple, and lead to spirited negotiations with your investors.

So instead, you opt to keep all ownership and finance your firm through debt. Your lender could be a bank, a private lender, a BDC, or the bond market. In so doing you take on a major fixed cost: debt payments must be made regularly, even though it may be months—or years—before your firm earns revenue, and that revenue is likely to be quite variable for years to come. Furthermore, to hedge against this risk your lender may demand that you pledge personal assets as collateral, putting your bank accounts and your house at risk in the event of default.

Not surprisingly, firms employ a mixed strategy, with that mix changing over the firm's life cycle. At a very early stage, debt is the dominant financing. After the firm proves the business concept (develops a prototype and/or makes its first sales), the next stage financing may be equity. But fairly early on, investors will be resistant to diluting their ownership with further equity offerings, so debt may again loom larger.

Besides the firm's life stage, other factors matter that aren't firm-specific. Three are particularly important:

- <u>The tax code</u>. Corporate expenses, including debt service, are tax deductible. The cost of equity isn't a visible cost, so it doesn't receive tax preference. The tax code biases firms in favor of debt, as it does homeowners.
- <u>Stock prices</u>. High stock prices offer firms larger amounts of investment for a given number of shares, so equity offerings (IPOs) rise in bull markets and fall in bear markets.

- Interest rates. Debt issued when interest rates are low is easier to service than when rates are high.

Integrating all three of these, in the years after the 2008–2009 meltdown many firms increased their bond issuance (which is tax deductible) and used the funds to buy back their stock, which they deemed underpriced after the 2008 market crash. The overall effect was to greatly increase the debt share of their capital structure.

The Cost of Capital: WACC

The right discount rate to compute an investment's NPV is the rate of return investors can expect from the best alternative investment of similar risk. Heretofore we have assumed that investment was either another stock or another bond/loan.

What if the firm finances itself with a mix of debt and equity? The answer is simple: use a discount rate that combines the two required rates of return in the debt/equity proportions in its capital mix. This computed discount rate is known as the *weighted average cost of capital, or* WACC:

> **WACC** = (DR of equity x % of capital from equity) + (DR of debt x % of capital from debt)

Ideally, the weights on the two components of capital structure should be based on their market values, not their book values. Their weights must sum to 100%, by definition.

As an example, if a firm has undertaken $300 million in debt and has $200 million in stockholder's equity, debt would be weighted 60% of capital and equity 40%.

Conceivably, the firm might be financed with multiple types of either capital source (debt or equity), or both. Its debt structure might include bonds of several different maturities and YTMs. Its shares might come in several different classes (e.g., common and preferred) offering different returns. In this case, compute WACC across all of these, using each class' respective proportion of total paid in capital.

The Promise and Problems of Leverage

Using "leverage" is the act of borrowing part of the price of a purchased asset. Let's use a home mortgage as an illustration.

Say you purchase a $500,000 house, making a down payment of $100,000 and taking out a mortgage (borrowing) the other $400,000. Your house is capitalized (financed) 20% with equity (your down payment) and 80% with debt. You have "levered" 4 to 1—$4 in debt for each dollar in equity.

If your equity comes from selling stocks that were earning a 10% return and your mortgage charges a 5% interest rate, then your WACC is:

$$20\% \times 10\% + 80\% \times .05 = 6\%.$$

If the house doubles in price to $1 million, your mortgage lender sees no additional return—they are strictly a lender. As the asset's owner, you enjoy all $500,000 in return. Your ROI is $500,000/$100,000 – 1, or 400%. That's why it is called "leverage"—the debt magnifies the impact (the ROI) of a change in the asset's value. (In the UK, leverage is often known as "gearing.")

Unfortunately, leverage magnifies price swings in downward as well as upward directions. Say your house fell in price by $100,000—from $500K to $400K. Again the lender wouldn't be exposed: the owner (you) would bear the brunt. In this case, a 20% drop in price would cause a 100% drop in your equity. **Leverage works in both directions**.

Growing firms may find it sensible to increase their leverage (gear up), but they can be caught by surprise if their growth unexpectedly reverses, such as in a recession.

A firm's leverage exposure can be measured in several ways. The most common are

- **The debt ratio:** the percentage of total capital that comes from debt; this is 80% in the house example.
- **Debt to equity ratio:** this is 4.0 in the above example.

Leverage can enhance a firm's value, up to a point of unsustainability. Thereafter, investors will raise their risk premium to reflect the prospect of missed payments or outright default. The resulting suppression of the firm's value is sometimes known as the **present value of prospective distress**.

Debt Distress

Debtholders can be patient when their borrowers run into trouble, but that patience isn't limitless. As a borrower takes on more debt, lenders will respond by withdrawing their loan or demanding a bigger risk premium (tougher terms). The borrower can enter a death spiral where each new borrowing comes at a higher price. A very visible example of this is Greece.

Estimating the specific cost of excess debt is beyond the score of this book. There are, however, numerous proxy measures that can alert firm managers and investors to impending trouble:

- Debt ratings. The rating agencies Standard & Poor's (S&P), Moody's and Fitch each employ analysts who examine borrowers' ability to service their debts, rating those debts on a scale similar to academic grades. Each rater uses a slightly different scale, but each has several levels of investment grade and speculative grade debt. Rating agencies closely examine debt ratios such as debt to total capital (debt plus equity). Investors require lower rated debt to offer higher YTMs.

- Risk premia. Financial markets track "spreads" between a given bond and a risk-free, or less risky, rate. Spreads are the incremental interest required in the market. Rising spreads indicate growing investor concern about repayment. European sovereign (government) bonds are often quoted in terms of their spread over German bunds, generally seen as the least risky in the EU.
- Interest coverage ratios. Analysts can compare a firm's annual earnings to its debt service payment, to assess how affordable those payments are. Mortgage lenders do the same when they review an application: typically they will only accept borrowers whose debt service will require no more than 30 or 35% of their gross income i.e., their income is at least 3x the debt service cost.

There rarely are universal thresholds for any of these indicators; they vary by industry and by a firm's maturity. For example, a capital-intensive, mature industry such as paper may rely heavily on long-term debt such that it accounts for one-third of its total liabilities, whereas retail (which often has low real estate costs because they lease their stores) may have a long-term debt ratio only half as high.

More broadly, investors seek companies that are capital efficient: that generate significant profits per dollar invested. The most common measure of this is return on equity (ROE), or profits divided by stockholder's equity. But investors know that companies can increase ROE simply by shrinking their equity base. So analysts sometimes rely on broader measures such as return on assets or return on capital. Each is a ratio of profits divided by assets or total capital.

XVII. Corporate Control

The Agency Problem

In all but the smallest firms, owners do not make most management decisions. Instead they hire agents—managers—to manage day-to-day operations. Shareholders exercise oversight through a board of directors. The board may make major decisions of strategic significance, but its role is governance, not management. It delegates management decisions to the chief executive and other corporate officers.

When owners are also managers, there is no conflict of interest, because every management decision is being made by an owner. This is no longer true when ownership and management are separated. Executives may pursue agendas inimical to shareholder value. For example, if executive bonuses are based on firm sales, the managers will have an interest in maximizing sales, even if some of the sales aren't profitable (and therefore reduce the firm's value). This is known as the "agency problem": agents need to be incented so that they make decisions in owners' interests—that is, that increase shareholder value.

Stock options have long been used to incent value-maximizing behavior. Many senior executives in large corporations today receive far less than half of their total compensation in cash. The remainder are in stock options: rights to buy stock at a specified price, which typically are good for several years. If the market price of the stock rises above the strike price of the option, executives will exercise their options—buy shares at the strike price—which will instantly be worth more than they paid. At a minimum, executives have an interest in acting to increase the firm's stock price above their option's strike price.

Even better is to make executives outright owners. Some firms offer grants of stock as part of compensation. Typically, these grants vest—become the recipient's property—over several years. This both encourages decisions that will benefit the firm long term and encourages the executive to remain an employee (vesting usually stops when employment ceases).

Mergers and Acquisitions (M&A)

Firms that are independent of each other may seek to combine. To do so, a majority of the shareholders in both firms must approve a merger resolution. When Firm A wishes to merge with Firm B, it may offer a price per share well above the market price of Firm B's stock to induce B's shareholders to approve the merger. Premiums of 30% over market aren't uncommon. Investment banks (I-banks) are often involved, advising either party on terms, or brokering relationships among acquirers and targets. M&A is one of the most lucrative practices in a typical I-bank.

Mergers are generally touted for their "synergies," premised on the belief that combining two firms will increase sales or lower costs per share. Considerable research has demonstrated this is the exception, not the rule. Although mergers can unquestionably reduce duplicative costs, they often disappoint. The most common problems are difficulties integrating IT systems and mismatches among the corporate cultures of the combined firms.

Finally, finance academics are skeptical of diversification-driven mergers. They argue that individual shareholders can achieve identical diversification by simply holding shares in both independent companies, so the considerable transaction costs and hassles of integration—not to mention the investment banking and legal fees—are largely wasted.

Corporate Restructurings

While firms buy and sell assets all the time, moves of broader strategic significance are known as restructurings. They can come in several guises:

- Acquisition of major assets, or whole firms
- Spin-offs of divisions into independent companies
- Major changes in capital structure, such as increases in leverage (debt) or in shares outstanding (equity); or the reverse
- Changes in ownership, such as buyouts by private investors (e.g., private equity firms), or the corporation's own managers (usually through extensive leverage)

Many buyouts, whether by managers, outsiders, or both, are financed with considerable debt, leading to the descriptive 1980s term "leveraged buyout," or LBO. (Management buyouts were sometimes called MBOs.) In the popular view such buyouts have a very bad reputation: acquirers are accused of "looting" the company's assets and slashing costs, including payroll, to meet extravagant debt service requirements. Proponents argue that the new owners typically believe they can manage the firm's assets more productively—i.e., earn a better return—than the incumbent owners and managers.

While there have been plenty of disasters as well as successes, research suggests that on average such restructurings have increased returns modestly, with little overall impact on employment. Private equity firms make their money by purchasing underperforming companies and reforming management practices in preparation for selling the firm at a profit—sometimes to another firm, more often in a public listing.

Consolidating Competitors

Although only whispered about, it seems clear that some mergers are intended to reduce competition in an industry. Under antitrust law the federal government is empowered to maintain competition by blocking mergers that would excessively consolidate market share in an industry or segment. But it isn't uncommon for merging parties to argue that their consolidation is necessary to defend against a previous consolidation by other competitors, suppliers, or customers.

M&A and restructuring activity tends to be cyclical, rising in bull markets and peaking around peaks in stock prices. One probable reason for this timing is affordability: companies can use high-priced stock to buy assets, or as collateral for increased debt. High stock prices may lower the standards of acquirers and diminish the quality of buyouts.

II Summary of Part II

Acquiring Capital

Why Firms Need Capital/How They Acquire Capital

(1) Firms have expenses before they have revenues: in their startup phase, and under full operations unless their customers pay immediately. Some capital expenditures (capex) is necessary for working capital, innovation, and growth.

(2) Firms can secure loans (debt) or sell partial ownership (equity). Equity has no explicit immediate cost, but it dilutes ownership. Debt does not sacrifice ownership, but it imposes a fixed cost because it must be serviced.

Debt Financing

(3) Many firms issue bonds that can be traded among investors. Bonds pay a fixed coupon payment expressed as an interest rate: a percent of par value. A $1,000 bond paying a 4% coupon would pay out $40 per year.

(4) The bond's yield is based on several factors:

a. Risk: Sketchier issuers must offer a higher interest rate than safe ones. Rating agencies track changes in issuers' riskiness.

b. Maturity: Longer maturities usually offer a higher interest rate than shorter ones. (The yield curve summarizes the pattern of yields for escalating maturities.)

(5) Because bonds' coupons are fixed, changes in circumstance don't change the coupon; rather, they change the bond's price. If a bond's price falls by 50%, its yield effectively doubles because the same size coupon is twice as large as a percentage of a bond whose price has halved.

(6) A bond's price is the present value of all of its future cashflows: interest payments and principal repayment at maturity. Its yield to maturity (YTM) is the discount rate that generates the bond's current market price. So while bonds' interest payments are fixed, their prices can vary.

(7) A rise in interest rates will depress the price of a preexisting bond if its YTM is below market rates. The reverse is true for a rate drop vis-à-vis a bond with an above-market interest rate.

(8) The investor can assure predictable cashflows by holding a bond until maturity—they are assured of getting all coupon payments, plus principal. In the meantime, they may have paper losses or gains depending on the bond's interest rate relative to market.

(9) Longer-maturity bonds are more sensitive to interest rate swings because any disparity vs. market rates will persist longer—i.e., above- or below-market cashflows will continue until maturity. One measure of comparative sensitivity is duration: the midpoint in the stream of cashflows that a bond returns. A traditional bond's duration is higher than half of its term, because its largest cashflow is its last one: the return of principal at maturity.

(10) Financial engineers have created variations on traditional bonds:

a. Zero coupon bonds have no interest payments, only a principal repayment at maturity.

b. Strips offer only coupon payments and no principal repayment.

c. Both of these trade at a greater discount to par than a traditional bond, because each only offers part of its cashflow stream.

d. A strip and a zero together are equivalent to a traditional bond.

Equity Financing

(11) At early stages, firms often raise equity privately, in private placements or from venture capitalists. If the firm does well it will eventually need greater amounts of capital, and will seek to list publicly. This is an initial public offering, or IPO.

(12) IPOs are generally facilitated by investment banks (for a hefty fee). Public listing allows a stock to trade on an exchange, making it very liquid and attractive to a wide range of investors.

(13) At each of these stages, the company will be valued so that each share can be valued.

(14) A firm's value is the present value of its future earnings. An investor directly enjoys earnings in two forms: current earnings may be paid out in dividends, and future earnings are reflected in capital gains upon the sale of their stock. Valuation PV computations produce an estimate of intrinsic value.

(15) "Value" investors estimate intrinsic value and compare it to the current market price. If the market price is higher, the stock is overpriced. If temporary conditions have driven prices below intrinsic value, the stock is a bargain.

(16) The originator of value investing Ben Graham argued that your intrinsic value estimate will always be rough and error-prone, so it is best to wait until the market price offers a "margin of safety."

(17) There are "hybrid" financing options that are mixes of debt and equity, such as preferred stock and convertible preferreds.

Capital Structure

(18) Firms choose the mix of debt and equity through which they finance themselves. This is not a one-time choice: it must be made continuously as conditions change.

(19) For example, a firm may borrow money (e.g., by issuing bonds) to buy back stock. This increases the debt portion of their capital structure and shrinks the equity portion. Many firms are presently taking advantage of rock-bottom interest rates to do this.

(20) The right discount rate to use for internal investment analysis is the weighted average cost of capital (WACC), which combines the cost of debt and the cost of equity in the proportions in the firm's capital structure.

(21) Leverage—increased use of other people's money—magnifies returns, both positive and negative. As debt service costs rise, creditors may become concerned about the borrower's ability to repay. This can affect the interest rate they charge, or the company's stock price. Profits can be depressed by these "costs of financial distress."

Corporate Control

(22) Owners' "agents" (corporate managers) may pursue their own self-interests, rather than shareholders'. Aligning owners' and agents' incentives is essential to maximizing shareholder wealth. Most alignment approaches give agents some ownership.

(23) Companies may wish to buy or sell divisions or whole companies for a variety of reasons, including consolidating competitors, diversification, and restructuring.

(24) In recent years a number of public companies have gone private—they have been purchased by firms that specialize in improving companies in order to sell them at a profit (to another private buyer, or in an IPO).

(25) Such restructurings commonly entail great increases in leverage to finance the purchase price. Critics argue that the debt burden, along with purchaser's greed, leads to mass layoffs and gutting of the restructured company. While this has undoubtedly occurred sometimes, the evidence suggests that most restructured companies have lower costs and earn higher returns than before the change.

Part III

Investing Capital

XVIII. Why Intrinsic Value and Market Prices Can Diverge: How Efficient Are Financial Markets?

If estimating the value of a company is so straightforward, why are stock prices volatile?

One reason is, of course, that different evaluators may use different assumptions. They may differ in their earnings forecasts or in the opportunity costs they use to discount those earnings. But it seems unlikely that deviations in prices are due solely to technical disagreements. Stock prices can move by more than 10% in a few days; it seems unlikely that such assumptions change so quickly.

Let's step back for a moment to ask what we mean by "volatility." The classic statistical measure of variation is *variance*. Variance is the sum of the squared difference between each data point and the mean for all the data points in the sample. (Squaring avoids having negative differences cancel out positive ones.) Working in squared units isn't intuitive, so "standard deviation" is the square root of variance. Standard deviation in a stock's returns is the common measure of volatility, or risk.

For many series of data points—such as daily changes in stock prices—their differences vs. their mean are "normally" distributed. A normal distribution is the famous bell curve, named after its shape. In a normal distribution about two-thirds of all points in the series are within one standard deviation above or below their mean. About 95% are within two standard deviations. Many companies' daily stock returns appear to follow a normal distribution. (However, analysts can mistakenly treat this common distribution as universally true. We will discuss this briefly later.)

Daily price changes may behave predictably as a group, but that does not make them predictable day by day. Statisticians have in fact found that stock prices behave randomly. Yesterday's change offers no useful predictions for today's. Finance academics are extremely skeptical of the value of so-called "technical analysis," or charting: attempting to divine future price movements from recent patterns.

The reason isn't surprising to anyone with a bit of knowledge of basic economics. If I see a situation that suggests a stock's price will rise, I have an incentive to buy it now, before the rise, so I can profit when the event occurs. In so doing I add to demand for that stock, which causes exactly what I predicted. When investors see an opportunity, their self-interest commands them to act, quickly, before others do. This process causes such opportunities to be fleeting: they close in a blink of an eye.

Fundamental Idea F: The Efficient Market Hypothesis

This process—where predictions about price movements become self-fulfilling due to the self-interest of investors—can make a market **efficient**. An "efficient market" is one where new information is incorporated quickly into asset prices. The more participants there are and the more liquid the market, the more efficient it should be.

The **efficient market hypothesis** (EMH) has existed for about fifty years, in three forms of escalating stringency:

1) The <u>weak form</u> posits that asset prices cannot be predicted using historical price or volume data (technical analysis).
2) The <u>semi-strong</u> form asserts that asset prices adjust quickly to any new public information such as company financial disclosures.
3) The <u>strong</u> form argues that prices immediately adjust to all information, including inside information.

Decades of research has suggested that one of these forms is almost certainly true in the stock market (scholars differ on which.). The most extensive work has examined the records of mutual fund managers, comparing active managers who choose specific stocks in order to "beat the market" vs. index funds, which simply hold all stocks in the index. Although in any single year about half of the active funds beat index funds, over long periods of time less than one in twenty do. Burton Malkiel's book *A Random Walk on Wall Street* first explained the EMH in very accessible form in the early 1970s; it has been published in over a dozen editions. The giant Vanguard mutual funds group was founded to make indexing widely available. Index funds have taken considerable market share from actively managed funds since the mid-2000s.

If the weak form is true, technical analysis is a fraud. If the semi-strong form is true, thousands of Wall Street analysts who pore over company financial reports aren't worth their giant salaries. If the strong form is true, those hedge fund managers who rely on inside information for an edge are risking jail for nothing.

Most finance academics consider the EMH an article of faith. I certainly believe that in the case of publicly traded US stocks the evidence is overwhelming. However, it cannot be denied that a handful of value investors have amassed impressive records outperforming indexes over the long term. A reasonable hypothesis is that a stronger form of EMH—perhaps the semi-strong form—occurs in large cap US stocks, while weaker forms occur in more thinly traded markets. In a market where inefficiencies create profit opportunities, investors will close those inefficiencies by simple pursuit of their self-interests.

Other Inefficiencies: Fear and Greed

So a market's efficiency probably correlates with its trading volume. Arbitrage opportunities (to buy an asset at one price and sell it at a higher price) will disappear quickly. How, then, do value investors beat the odds? Discipline and patience.

Anyone with investing experience has witnessed markets overreacting to news, both positive and negative. Market bubbles occur when an initial positive development (like a new invention) drives up the price of a stock, and thereafter other investors continue to buy it, simply because its price has already risen. Similar momentum investing can also occur on bad news.

Value investors realize, therefore, that **market prices can diverge from intrinsic value**—simply due to investors' emotions and herd behavior. Legendary investors like Buffett develop their own estimate of a company's intrinsic value and wait until its market price falls well below it.

Of course, any estimate of intrinsic value is just that—an estimate. Buffett's mentor Benjamin Graham taught the importance of seeking a "margin of safety": buy only when the market price is well below intrinsic value. A handful of value investors like Buffett and Bill Ruane of Sequoia Fund have built enviable long-term records; some argue this disproves the EMH. My position is that because nineteen of twenty stock pickers cannot outperform the index, some form of EMH certainly operates in the American stock market.

Fat Tails

Statisticians theorize that bell curves may not capture the true variability of stock returns. A simple change to a distribution with "fat tails" can significantly increase the frequency of very unusual events. This argument was often made in the aftermath of the 2008 meltdown, when banks' risk models greatly underestimated its chances.

XIX. Fundamental Idea G: Portfolio Construction: The Capital Assets Pricing Model (CAPM) and the Modern Portfolio Theory (MPT)

We have noted the significantly different risks among several asset classes such as stocks and bonds. The risk tolerance of most individuals, and firms, changes as their circumstances change. An example is an individual investing for retirement. Early in their life their assets should be concentrated in stocks or stock funds, which historically have offered the highest return, and also have a high standard deviation. Stocks have almost never had negative returns for a full decade, so an individual who does not need to spend their investments for several decades has ample time to recover from a bad market.

Things are very different for a retiree, or someone whose retirement is imminent. Their weekly spending depends on the value of their investments. They have far less tolerance of volatility.

This suggests a portfolio approach throughout an individual's lifespan: allocate your investments among both stocks and bonds, changing the mix over time— heavy in stocks in your twenties; heavy in bonds in your seventies. Firms may face analogous choices for investing their liquid reserves, depending on their need for those reserves as affected by capex opportunities and the industry's maturity.

(The above outline of retirement planning is extremely simplified. For a more detailed and nuanced treatment, see my book with Riaan Nel: It's the *INCOME, Stupid! The 7 Secrets of a Stress-Free Retirement*.)

The general notion is that **investors should construct a portfolio including several asset classes to modulate their risk**. This acknowledges that risk reduction probably means return reduction, too.

Modern Portfolio Theory (MPT) is a framework for designing portfolios. Implemented fully, it can allow an investor to **optimize** their portfolio, to achieve the highest possible expected return for given level of risk, or minimize risk while achieving a target return. A companion book *Hedge Fund Secrets* (with Tucker Balch) covers the techniques in more detail; we will simply introduce portfolio construction here.

Risk and Return, Again

Finance academics array any asset in risk/return space. The common framework, developed in the Capital Assets Pricing Model (CAPM), is like that shown in figure 5-1. Return is defined as the change in an asset's value over a specified time period (typically daily or annually), and risk is the standard deviation of those returns. Figure 5-1 arrays a number of asset classes in rough risk/return order. For example, long-term bonds' annual returns have averaged about 5 to 6% with about 5%

standard deviation. This means that in about 95% of years, bond returns could vary between -4% to +16%. (The edges of this range are two standard deviations above and below the 5–6% annual mean.) Although bond interest payments are fixed, prices are not, which explains the occasional negative returns.

Stocks, by contrast, have averaged about 10% returns, with about a 20% standard deviation. This means that in most years annual stock returns were between -30% and +50%.

A portfolio constructed of a mix of these assets will have average returns that are a weighted combination of the individual asset's returns, in weights based on each asset's portfolio proportion. Using the returns and risk above, a 50/50 stock/bond portfolio—common in balanced mutual funds—would have the following characteristics:

Portfolio average return: .50 x 10% + .50 x 5% = 7.5%

Portfolio standard deviation: .50 x 20% + 50 x 5% = 12.5%

Most of the time its returns would fall in a range between -12.5% and +32.5% (two standard deviations around 7.5%).

An MPT analyst would connect the asset classes at the highest return for each level of risk. The classes on that curve dominate any others that offer lower returns for the same risk. MPT analysts call the curve connecting these dominating asset classes the **efficient frontier**. Figure 5-1 was a simplified example of one.

Diversification

Having all of your eggs in one basket is a terrific way to get very rich. Most of the world's richest individuals have heavily concentrated their investments. Buffett for example invests more than 50% of Berkshire's portfolio in only three or four stocks. Bill Gates concentrated entirely in Microsoft and became the world's richest person (until he gave much of his wealth away to found his eponymous foundation.)

Of course, most failed investors have concentrated, too. Concentration is a fine policy, if you can be sure you will stay lucky. For the rest of us, some degree of diversification is prudent. It will slow your climb to billionaire status, but it will prevent your pauperization.

Finance academics have determined that there are significant benefits to diversification. But as with so many other things, diversification has diminishing returns: Beyond fifteen to twenty positions, a portfolio reaches an irreducible minimum standard deviation (risk). That minimum is the standard deviation of the market as a whole. **You can largely eliminate company-specific (individual) risk via diversification, but you cannot eliminate market (systematic) risk**.

Improving on a Simple Portfolio

As we discussed in chapter XI, firms may diversify to become less subject to their home industry's economic cycle. But we noted in chapter XVI that the firm's shareholders can diversify more efficiently within their own portfolios. We will now elaborate.

Recall the example from chapter XI of an oil company that wished to diversify by buying into an airline: one would perform well when oil prices are high, and one when they are low. The statistical term for this relationship is **correlation**. The **correlation coefficient** between two items can range between -1.0 and +1.0. A coefficient of -1.0 indicates that the two items move in opposite directions; a +1.0 correlation indicates they move in the same direction. Generally these relationships stem from a third factor that affects both items. In the case of the oil company and airline, it is oil prices: the oil company's stock price is positively correlated with oil prices and the airline is negatively correlated with oil prices, so they are negatively correlated with each other.

An investor can reduce his or her portfolio's volatility by choosing components (individual positions) with low or (ideal but rare) negative correlation.

Expanding on the Correlation Idea: Modern Portfolio Theory (MPT)

We've seen that a portfolio of several issues has an expected return and risk that is a weighted average of those of its components. If those components have low—or ideally, negative—correlations—it may be possible to reduce risk *without* a comparable drop in return.

Is it possible to *optimize* a portfolio? That is, can it be designed to maximize returns within a specified risk ceiling? Or can the mirror image be created: a portfolio that minimizes risk subject to a return floor?

Portfolio optimization is covered in some detail in *What Hedge Funds Really Do*, but we can summarize here. Any optimization problem has four main components:

- Decision variables: the things you are choosing among—in this case, the percentage of the portfolio in each position.
- An objective function: a goal that you wish to either maximize (e.g., return) or minimize (e.g., risk).
- A constraint: a floor or ceiling on the acceptable outcome. Risk might be subject to ceiling, or return to a floor. This determines the feasible set of decision variable values.
- A search algorithm: An efficient way to search through all the possible combinations of decision variables to find the one that achieves the optimal value of the objective function, while staying within the specified constraints.

Linear programming is a common optimization technique if all functions (objective and constraints) are linear. Nonlinear programming techniques also exist. All are beyond this book's scope. We will concentrate on a simpler approach.

Optimal Mixes of Risk and Return: The Sharpe Ratio

What we wish for is the portfolio that offers the highest return per unit of risk, subject to a return floor or risk ceiling. This is a version of "bang for the buck." William Sharpe developed a measure that is easily computable: the **Sharpe ratio**.

The Sharpe ratio is computed for each position. Its numerator is the position's excess return over the risk-free return. Its denominator is the position's standard deviation. The numerator is a value you wish to maximize, and the denominator is one you wish to minimize. Sharpe ratios of 1.0 imply that the investor's return and risk are about balanced. A higher Sharpe ratio indicates a superior return-to-risk relationship. Most real assets have Sharpe ratios well below 1.0.

In terms of the efficient frontier, Sharpe ratios can be displayed in the same return/risk space. The feasible set—the range of choices that are not constrained away—limits choices to those above any specified return ceiling and above the specified risk floor. Each ratio is a ray (line) extending up and to the right of the risk-free return (currently close to zero); the ray's slope is its Sharpe ratio. The portfolio on the efficient frontier within the feasible set that intersects with the highest Sharpe ratio's ray is the optimum.

ABCs: Alphas, Betas, and Correlations

Since the efficient market hypothesis (EMH) suggests that most investors are better off indexing—buying and holding the entire market through an index fund or ETF—it is reasonable to examine each position's correlations to the market as a whole. The MPT framework regresses a stock's daily returns (on the Y-axis) against the market's daily returns (on the X-axis). Generally, they are highly positively correlated, so a scatterplot will run diagonally on a Southwest to Northeast direction. (For a 1.0 correlation, all points of daily returns would fall on a 45-degree line. More commonly, they are a scattering tightly grouped around that line.)

All regression lines are described by two coefficients, alpha and beta. Alpha is the Y-intercept of the regression line, and beta is the line's slope. MPT interprets these as follows:

- **Alpha** is the stock's average return relative to the market. Investment managers "seek alpha": they aim to offer systematically higher returns than passive investing. That is, they wish to outperform their benchmark.
- **Beta** is the stock's volatility relative to the market. If the slope of the stock's regression line is 1.5, it means that on average the stock's price will rise or fall

1.5x as much as the market. Betas are computed frequently for all stocks and are easily available on investor sites such as Yahoo Finance. Volatile tech stocks may have betas of 2.0 or more, while stable utilities may be well under .50.

A portfolio's alpha and beta are likewise the weighted average of those of its components. Portfolios that include shorts—betting against a stock—will have components with negative weights.

Correlations are reflected in the degree of tightness of the regression line.

The core idea of MPT is that a stock's return and risk can be decomposed into two elements: market return and risk, plus those of the specific stock.

Conclusion

Modern Portfolio Theory is a framework for combining individual positions, estimating its risk and return, and optimizing its design. Portfolios can eliminate individual risk, but not market risk, through diversification. A portfolio's risk and return are that of the weighted average of its components. However, risk can be reduced further if the portfolio components are uncorrelated.

Portfolios can be optimized to achieve at least a floor level of return within a ceiling level of risk. Optimization techniques such as linear programming can do this very efficiently.

The core idea of MPT is that a stock's return and risk can be decomposed into two elements: market return and risk, plus those of the specific stock.

XX. Financial Markets and Careers

Throughout the book we have referred to "financial markets" as places where firms can acquire capital and investors can deploy capital. But what exactly are these markets? What is traded within them? And—more important—how can you make a living there?

The Economic Role of Financial Markets

A "market" is a place—real or virtual—where buyers and sellers exchange: buyers offer money in exchange for sellers' goods or services. Households save part of their income for future needs. They invest their savings in financial instruments: stocks, bonds, savings accounts, certificates of deposit (CDs), etc. The financial markets (colloquially, Wall Street, the lower Manhattan district where many markets are headquartered) match up households' savings with investment opportunities. Economists generally believe that market exchange—where both buyers and sellers pursue their respective self-interests—allocate resources (in this case, savings) more efficiently than any other mechanism. So the financial industry's economic role is to allocate capital efficiently in the broader economy.

The industry isn't above taking for itself a healthy cut of the revenue from these transactions. Industry occupations have a deserved reputation of being very well-compensated. In the years before the 2008 crash, Wall Street employed less than 5% of the labor force, yet enjoyed about half of all corporate profits. Pundits can debate whether Wall Street's social contribution is commensurate with its generous salaries. For our purpose, we will merely outline how the skills you've gained through this book can be used in your career. This chapter will mention some classic financial roles. The final chapter will broaden the discussion to show how "non-financial types" can nevertheless differentiate themselves through financial acumen.

Financial Institutions

We will divide this vast sector into three main segments: retail, exchange, and management institutions.

Retail Institutions

Your first encounter with a retail financial institution was probably a bank branch. Banks' core business model is interest rate arbitrage: borrowing money at one rate and lending it out at a higher rate. From a bank's perspective, your savings or checking account is a short-term loan—short-term because you can withdraw it with no notice.

Banks use their capital to make loans: auto loans, home mortgages, and business loans. They may securitize these loans—combine many streams of debt service payments into a bond that is floated to public investors.

Banks are the most visible customer-facing institutions that traffic in debt. The two key retail institutions that traffic in equity are brokerage firms and mutual funds. Brokerage firms—stockbrokers—execute trades in publicly traded stock on major exchanges on behalf of their clients, charging a commission for each share traded. Since their revenues scale with trading volume, many stockbrokers present themselves as advisers who can suggest trades for you. Brokerage firms can be full-service, where a client is assigned a particular person to take their orders and perhaps offer advice; or discount, where staff is much leaner and the client mainly trades online or through an 800 number.

Mutual funds: Active vs. passive management (indexing)

Mutual funds came into existence to allow retail investors to diversify even if they could invest only limited capital. Consider that if about twenty stocks are needed to minimize individual risk, round lots of stock are one hundred shares each, and stock prices average (say) $30 per share, an individual would need $60,000 (20 positions x $30/share x 100 shares) to build a diversified portfolio. That is far beyond the means of many investors.

Mutual funds pool the capital from many investors to buy blocks of stock to create diversification. (Bond funds followed soon thereafter.) Clients buy shares in the fund, so they do not own its stocks directly; rather, they own a proportional share of the fund's portfolio.

The original mutual funds were stock funds, where their managers attempted to choose the fund's holdings to outperform the overall market—to "beat the market." As noted in earlier chapters, this goal proved remarkably elusive. So by the mid-1970s widely available stock index funds were offered, first by Vanguard, and later by most other fund companies.

This distinction between "active management" (stock-picking) and passive management (indexing) is fundamental. For decades, finance academics were puzzled that index funds' market share grew so slowly and active management remained dominant. Then 2008 happened. Stock prices fell about 60% from peak to the March 2009 trough, and all stock funds were hurt. But active funds suffered no less than index funds, even though active funds' raison d'être was that their superior stock selection would limit drawdowns in a market crash. When active funds disappointed so dramatically, investors began to emigrate. Inflows into index funds have roughly equaled outflows from active funds, so index funds' market share has now overtaken active funds.

Since retail operations are very labor intensive, these types of institutions constantly need new talent. We will discuss career paths later in this chapter.

Exchange Institutions

When a bank, brokerage firm, or mutual fund takes your money, it usually deploys it through an exchange. Exchanges are designated markets in which trading in a particular security takes place. The best-known one is the New York Stock Exchange (NYSE), but there are scores of regional stock exchanges throughout the world. In addition, private exchanges, sometimes known as "dark pools," exist for buyers and sellers who wish to avoid a public exchange's transaction costs.

Despite the dramatic movie scenes of specialists furiously trading on the floor of the stock exchange, little human activity occurs there anymore; most trading is now electronic. Exchange careers are limited, except perhaps for IT and telecommunications. *What Hedge Funds Really Do* describes the operations of major exchanges.

Management Institutions

The largest salaries are in wealth management and related occupations, although the largest number of workers are in retail roles. Wealth management organizations design and manage portfolios on behalf of clients, or advise clients on such decisions.

These institutions are generally classified by the type of financial instruments they specialize in, the types of clients they work with, or the types of strategies they employ. Mutual funds are management institutions for retail investors: they pool individuals' funds and manage a collective portfolio. (Even indexing requires some management, to adjust the portfolio when the index changes.) Hedge funds are also investment pools only available to "accredited" investors—those with enough wealth they are presumed to take care of themselves. Hedge funds range in their strategies that partly overlap with mutual funds. The pass-through entities mentioned in chapter XV likewise pool investors' capital to buy and manage portfolios of specific types of assets: real estate for REITs, energy projects for MLPs, and small business loans for BDCs.

These entities all need a sales force to entice investors into placing their capital. They may share their mutual funds or fees with brokerage firms. In addition, financial advisers (often known as investment advisers) may earn a commission from them for steering clients to one of their products. Pass-through entities rely more on investment advisers, while mutual funds rely more on brokerage firms for their sales force.

Many investors that invest large sums have in-house managers. The best known are large endowments such as Harvard's or Yale's. Major foundations may likewise hire staff to manage their endowments. If they contract with management firms, they may hire investment consultants to advise them on their allocation among managers. Hedge "funds of funds" serve a similar role for groups of hedge funds:

clients invest in the fund of funds, which apportions capital among the hedge funds in its stable (and charges a fee on top of the hedge funds' already hefty fees).

Increasingly, firms that can make revenue from either commissions (such as brokerages) or management fees (such as managers and advisers) are shifting toward a fee-based model. Typically, the firm manages a client's assets and charges a fee based on the value of the assets under management (AUM). Fees are generally about 1% of AUM, plus or minus. Managers who claim superior performance charge much higher fees. For example, the standard fee for both hedge funds and private equity funds is "two and twenty": 2% of AUM plus 20% of absolute return. However, because average performance in this industry has disappointed, fees are slipping.

Careers in the Financial Industry

Occupations in the industry generally fall into one of five types, plus one 'bot' that may replace some of these in the future.

Sales

The largest personnel need is for salespersons, who persuade investors to give them capital for the product or service they offer. Firms hire for personality and social skills, subject to an elementary financial literacy requirement. (Ex-college athletes are popular in financial sales roles.) These jobs go under many titles—financial consultant, financial adviser, client relations manager—but their core function is sales. These jobs are probably the most common first job for many in finance, but those who are ambitious seek to progress into one of the following occupations.

Journalism/Commentary

Not truly part of the financial industry, but close observers, are journalists and writers who comment on investing. They may approach it from a personal finance perspective (such as *Money* magazine) or cover news of the industry (such as *Institutional Investor*). Some journalists cover the industry's role in politics, more often from a political angle. Many of these are poorly trained in finance and have only a tenuous grasp of their subject. The handful of most impressive commentators typically had early experiences inside the industry.

A related occupation are newsletter writers who charge for investment analysis and advice.

Trading

Employees who are willing to make rapid decisions and who develop some instinct for market behavior can become traders: those who actively trade a part of a portfolio. The portfolio may be a client's, or it may be their own employer's (proprietary, or prop, trading). Most traders specialize in particular asset classes, such as utility stocks, short-term municipal paper, or junk bonds. Intuition, decisiveness, and speed are at a premium. Rewards can be great, but failures are swiftly punished. You are only paid well if you trade well. Traders are temperamentally risk-takers.

Technical

This embraces all functions that do not face customers but keep the business humming:

- Quants develop and program the computer algorithms (algos) that trade securities quickly and automatically. This both exploits and closes market inefficiencies. *Hedge Fund Secrets* was written for budding quants.
- IT and telecomm specialists manage the information and communications systems that allow a firm to trade. Many firms locate their servers as close to exchanges as possible. So much trading is done by algorithm (algo) that profit opportunities can vanish in milliseconds. Cutting the time to transmit an order can beat other algos to the trade. Michael Lewis' *Flash Boys* is an entertaining introduction to this competition to shave microseconds off trades.

Management

The greatest prestige, and usually the greatest rewards, go to those who make or advise on major investing decisions:

- Investment advisers/wealth managers act as the interface between retail clients and funds.
- Analysts follow particular securities (e.g., the stocks of specific companies), forecast earnings, and value the stock to make buy and sell recommendations to clients.
- Fund managers allocate portfolios to attempt to match (for passive funds) or beat (for active funds) their benchmark.

Generally, prestige and rewards escalate as you progress among these roles. They require virtuosity in the techniques described in this book as well as close attention to trends in the industry and the larger economy.

Roboadvisors

Automation has come to Wall Street no less than in most other industries, and on a similar trajectory: first prosaic back office functions were significantly automated, then higher-level functions also. Indexing is a very visible example: it eliminates the need for human judgement because the portfolio simply mimics its benchmark index. Automated portfolio advice and management is spreading rapidly and being embraced by a new generation of investors who do not find human advisers cost-effective. This trend will depress demand for many of the roles mentioned above like management and trading while increasing demand for technical roles. It will also reduce prices that can be charged by the survivors. As noted earlier, advisory and management fees are already falling in some segments of the industry.

Beyond these financial industry roles, financial proficiency can be useful to you in almost every occupation. That is the subject of the final chapter.

III Summary of Part III

Investing Capital

The Efficient Market

(1) Most asset prices seem to follow a random walk. There is no gain in searching for patterns.

(2) Therefore, many asset markets seem to be highly efficient: new information is incorporated into asset prices very quickly. The efficient market hypothesis (EMH) makes this explicit.

(3) A market's efficiency depends on its liquidity and trading volume. More trades mean more opportunities for investors to close opportunities created by inefficiencies, so inefficiency is self-correcting.

(4) EMH theorists identify three versions of the hypothesis: strong, semi-strong, and weak, depending on the range of information quickly included in asset prices. The largest and most liquid markets (like the NYSE) seem to conform to the strongest form of EMH.

(5) Strong forms of the EMH imply there is little to be gained from active investment management. Advocates argue that indexing is no less effective and far less expensive.

(6) There clearly are exceptions; the most common are a handful of value investors who have outperformed major benchmarks. This only disproves the EMH if their records are far more common than chance alone would suggest. The number of exceptions is minuscule, so EMH is still viable for now.

(7) Value investors use patience to wait until investors' emotions drive a stock's price below their estimate of intrinsic value—ideally far enough below to generate a margin of safety.

Modern Portfolio Theory

(8) Assets can be arrayed by their return and their risk to form an efficient frontier: the set of positions that dominate their alternatives—and that earn a higher return for the same risk, or have a lower risk for the same return.

(9) Most assets' returns are normally distributed (like a bell curve). The width of the distribution indicates its standard deviation—the variation in returns possible.

(10) Portfolios are collections of positions (investments). An investor can diversify away the individual risk of the companies in their portfolio with fifteen to twenty separate positions. They cannot diversify away market risk.

(11) A portfolio's return and risk is the weighted average of the returns and risks of each of its positions. The risk may be less than this average if the positions are poorly correlated with each other.

(12) Any stock's risk and return can be decomposed into two components: alpha, its average return relative to the market, and beta, its price change relative to the market.

(13) Portfolios can be optimized: investors can choose the percentage invested in each position in order to maximize return subject to a risk constraint (ceiling), or minimize risk subject to a return constraint (floor).

Financial Institutions and Careers

(14) The financial industry includes several segments, such as banks, brokerages, and funds. Financial rewards are considerable: Wall Street has earned profits out of proportion to its size for decades.

(15) The basic question a budding finance type needs to ask is: Am I technically proficient, or more of a people person? The former type goes into analysis, advice, and asset management. The latter goes into sales. Many careers start in sales, but those with strong financial acumen rarely stay there.

(16) In any case, growing automation of many functions is shrinking opportunities for all but the most technically competent workers. This trend, which began in manufacturing, has now arrived in finance. It will reduce hiring and shrink compensation for those who keep their jobs. Survivors will need to differentiate themselves: they cannot be cheaper than software, so they need to be better.

Part IV

Personal Applications and Conclusion

XXI. Personal Applications

Most of this book has dealt with finance in a business setting. But in the near term, chances are that you will first use your financial literacy on more personal decisions. This short chapter indicates the wide range available to you.

Committing to a Long-Term Contract

Many vendors offer you a fixed monthly price in lieu of charging per transaction. For example, Amazon Prime offers free shipping, plus other services, for a set fee per year. Compute how many times per year, or per month, you must use the service before its costs are less than the per-transaction pricing. If this payback period is longer than a year, compute present values to reflect the time value of money.

Buying or Leasing

You have amassed two or three thousand dollars toward your first new car. You choose the car you want, for which your savings cover only 10% of its total price. The friendly salesman offers you a chance to finance the car with a loan or a lease. How do you choose? Estimate the PV of each and choose the lower one. If you can pay cash for the whole car, include in your calculation the opportunity cost of depleting your savings.

Refinancing Your Mortgage

You have a mortgage on your home that you secured when rates were higher than they are now. You can refinance at a lower rate, but the transaction has fees associated with it (title insurance, lender's and broker's fees). How do you decide? Compute the NPV of the refinancing: negative cashflows are the transaction fees, and positive cashflows are the monthly interest savings. Decide if you are confident you will remain in the house longer than the refi's payback period. What will be the NPV if you hold the house as long as you foresee?

Saving Toward a Major Goal Like Retirement

Set a target level of spending in retirement that your savings must supply. Typically retirees wish to maintain their working lifestyle in retirement, so you may need to replace, say, about 90% of your working income. Social Security might supply 20%, leaving 70% that must come from savings. Say that is $70,000 for you.

How much must you save to produce a nest egg from which you can spend $70K per year without depleting it long before you die? Analysts suggest that spending 4% of your nest egg annually in retirement has a high probability of being sustainable for at least thirty years. (The unspent part remains invested, and some investment growth replaces your depletions.) That suggests a savings target of $70K/.04 = $1,750,000. (Gulp.) Take a spreadsheet and compute how much you must save each year for the next thirty to forty years until your retirement date. (Hint: it will probably be a much larger fraction of your salary than you'd planned.)

For much more on this problem, see *It's the INCOME, Stupid*!

XXII. Summary: What This Book Did, and *Didn't*, Include

This book was a very high-altitude introduction to finance. It focused on seven fundamental ideas:

- Fundamental Idea A: Time Value of Money—Chapter III
- Fundamental Idea B: Risk and Return/Diversification—Chapter V
- Fundamental Idea C: Net Present Value—Chapter VII
- Fundamental Idea D: Bond and Stock Prices—Chapters XIV and XV
- Fundamental Idea E: Capital Structure (Debt/Equity Mix)—Chapter XVI
- Fundamental Idea F: Efficient Market Hypothesis—Chapter XVIII
- Fundamental Idea G: Portfolio Construction (CAPM and MPT)—Chapter XIX

Let's recapitulate the basics of each. Of course, this book skipped a vast number of important finance topics in the interest of brevity. The final few sections will mention some of the most significant topics we excluded.

A) Time Value of Money—Chapter III

If you can invest $1 and a year later receive $1.10, you will be nearly indifferent between the two situations. In other words, to value an amount in the future equally to an amount in the present, the future value must be greater than the present value.

Much of finance entails projecting costs and benefits over a number of periods in the future. To be able to come to a decision about a stream of payments, we need to express value at different time periods in common units. If it takes more dollars in the future to be equivalent to a given number of dollars in the present, than the converse is also true: **We can convert a future value into a present value by discounting**.

Specifically, a future value is discounted at the rate of return the decisionmaker foregoes by investing in a project under consideration, for the number of years until that return will appear. Future values are discounted more if the opportunities foregone are lucrative (i.e., would earn a high return) or if they are far in the future.

Using the present value formula for different time periods—specifically, for an indefinite stream of regular payments, and a stream that is delayed for some number of years—allows quick computation of combined present values. These shortcuts are very helpful for term loans and similar calculations.

B) Risk and Return/Diversification–Chapter V

In general, there are no free lunches: **higher-return investments entail higher risk**. Investors demand a risk premium for riskier investments, which increases the discount rate used to value them.

To a degree, a portfolio can reduce risk to any individual position through diversification. But there are diminishing returns to diversification: **risk reduction peters out after a portfolio has about fifteen to twenty individual positions**. The remaining risk, market risk, cannot be diversified away.

C) Net Present Value—Chapter VII

All investing involves spending some money now to generate a larger amount of money later—to earn a positive return. So any investment needs to be evaluated by comparing the money it will generate to the money it will cost. Several simple shortcuts like payback (time until cumulative benefits equal costs) or ROI (benefits/costs – 1 for a specified time period) approach this, but they ignore some cashflows and entirely omit the time value of money.

The gold standard for investment analysis is net present value (NPV): the present value of all benefits minus that of all costs, each discounted appropriately. Positive NPV projects add value, while negative NPVs subtract value.

There can be great disagreements about key inputs to an NPV analysis. Low discount rates or long time periods (to generate benefits) produce higher NPVs. High discount rates and short benefit periods deflate NPVs.

Beyond being careful about assumptions, some elements of an NPV analysis are inherently uncertain, because they involve forecasting the future. Thoughtful analysts conduct sensitivity analysis, re-running the NPV computation several times under different scenario assumptions.

D) Bond and Stock Prices—Chapters XIV and XV

Stocks are equity investments: the investor is a part owner in the business and experiences all of its upsides and downsides. Bondholders are lenders: they are entitled only to debt service payments from the borrower. As a result, stock returns are significantly more volatile than bonds.

After you buy a bond, your cashflows are entirely predictable: a series of interest payments over time, then repayment of principal at maturity. Any events that could affect the bond, like changes in interest rates, do not affect these—they are fixed. Instead, they affect the price of the bond. For example, a rise in interest rates makes the fixed rate offered by the bond less attractive. The numerator of the bond's return—the coupon doesn't change; instead the denominator—the bond's price—does.

Bonds' sensitivity to interest rates scale with the bond's maturity. Longer maturities have more time for surprises to occur. Duration—the weighted average time to receive the bond's cashflows, including both interest and principal—roughly measures this sensitivity.

Price changes mean that a fixed coupon payment represents a changing bond yield. But a bond's values are entirely predictable, if you hold until maturity. Yield to maturity (YTM) is the discount rate at which the present value of those cashflows equals the current price of the bond. A falling bond price offers a rising YTM, and vice versa.

Stock pricing is very similar to bond pricing, with dividends substituting for coupon payments, and terminal/horizon value for principal repayment. However, stocks are ownership—hopefully in a company with rising prospects. A stock's intrinsic value, then, accounts for expected growth in either dividends or terminal value. It is the present value of all future cashflows.

Analysts commonly do not compute the value of a share of stock directly. Instead, to remind themselves they are valuing a real business, they value the corporation, then estimate share value by dividing by the number of shares outstanding.

E) Capital Structure (Debt/Equity Mix)—Chapter XVI

Firms choose their mix of debt and equity. Each has pros and cons.

Equity, which is the most common financing early in a firm's life cycle, is ownership. Founders sacrifice partial control to gain equity capital. Equity has no explicit cost; however, because it is riskier than debt, investors will require a risk premium. So the cost of equity to the firm is generally higher than debt.

Debt isn't ownership, so incumbent owners aren't diluted. However, debt service costs are a fixed cost that gets precedence over most other expenses (must be paid before most other creditors, such as suppliers or employees). Investors track the magnitude of a firm's debt burden and will penalize firms at risk of distress by demanding enhanced risk premiums. The risk of financial distress has a tangible cost.

Leverage—debt—can turbocharge returns, both up and down. Most firms do not leverage as much as markets allow, in order to avoid the risk of distress.

A firm's discount rate should be the weighted average of its debt and equity costs of capital—literally, its weighted average cost of capital, or WACC.

F) Efficient Market Hypothesis—Chapter XVIII

Markets exist to match buyers and sellers of the item being traded—in this case, capital. Markets allocate resources more efficiently than other schemes. Prices send signals to market participants to help them make decisions.

An "efficient" market is one where new information is incorporated in the price of assets quite quickly. Evidence is that most stock prices move randomly: there is no advantage to studying patterns in prices. This suggests the stock market may be highly efficient. The efficient market hypothesis (EMH) makes this assertion specific, and comes in several different forms of escalating rigor.

In such markets most effort to outperform market averages is wasted, and index investing becomes the superior strategy. Results of long-term comparisons of active and passive (index) investors mostly confirms this: **very few active investors outperform their benchmarks** over long periods (decades). However, a very few do. They do not discredit the EMH, but they do suggest that not all markets are purely efficient.

G) Portfolio Construction (CAPM and MPT)—Chapter XIX

Diversification can reduce the risks associated with any single stock. By the same principle, it makes sense to diversify across asset classes to distribute your investments, given the different risk/return characteristics of stocks and bonds. This is known as a **portfolio**.

Modern Portfolio Theory (MPT) is a framework for analyzing and designing portfolios. It distinguishes among classes of assets—stocks, bonds, REITs, etc.—by their average return and their risk (the volatility, or standard deviation, of that average return).

A portfolio's risk and return characteristics are the weighted averages of those of each of its components (individual positions). Portfolio design chooses those proportions. An optimized portfolio chooses proportions that maximize expected return subject to a risk constraint (ceiling), or minimize risk subject to a return constraint (floor).

In portfolio design there are occasional free lunches: if portfolio components are relatively uncorrelated, it is possible to lower risk without decreasing return.

Portfolios can be optimized, to maximize return for a tolerable risk level; or to minimize risk for a tolerable minimal return. The best approach involves programming methods beyond this book's scope. But a simple approach is the Sharpe ratio: return divided by risk. Of the portfolio options available on the efficient frontier, the one with the highest Sharpe ratio is generally optimal.

What This Book *Didn't* Cover

Being a very high-level introduction, this book omitted many important elements of these topics. Below is a very incomplete list of interesting items I omitted, to give you a sense of what more you can learn by expanding your finance knowledge further.

- Time value of money: How do psychological factors and incentives affect an investor's discount rate? For example, do politicians' term limits make them less concerned about the long run—i.e., does it raise their implicit discount rate?
- NPV and benefit/cost analysis: Does NPV really capture the essence of a decision when benefits and costs are in different units? How might it bias a decision; say, in favor of large or near-term projects?
- Risk, diversification, and WACC: Since portfolio positions do not have identical risk, should they be sized equally? Or should position sizes be risk-weighted? What weights should be used to compute WACC: balance sheet or market proportions?
- Sensitivity analysis: How can an investment analysis identify the specific uncertainties to which a decision is most sensitive, so the analyst can know where to devote his efforts to reduce uncertainty?
- Optimal liquid asset holdings: Firms recently have been retaining far more cash (or liquid securities) than simple finance suggests is prudent. Do we need to reconsider our thoughts about capital structure on the asset side of the balance sheet, as this book explained for the liability side? What factors drive these corporate decisions? Should we change any of those in our control, such as tax policy?
- Finance needs in the life cycle: How has the optimal capital structure over firms' lifespans changed throughout history? Do we need to change any of our institutions to make it easier for firms, especially startups, to acquire capital?
- Stock and bond pricing: Do we need to replace the dividend discount model in a world of ultralow dividends? Do we need a new bond pricing model for variable rate bonds?
- Capital structure: If excessive leverage is risky, why did so many banks practice it prior to 2008? Did the post-meltdown regulatory attempts to limit leverage, like Dodd-Frank, make the financial system less risky?
- Efficient markets: What are the major exceptions to the EMH, and what can we learn from them? What are the downsides of the recent migration to indexing by individual investors? Will the market shares of active and passive investing strategies oscillate in cycles?
- Portfolio design: What are the tools portfolio managers use to optimize?

This book only gave you a taste of the challenges available in finance to those with ambitions. Now that you've sampled an appetizer, I hope you are interested in a full meal.

XXIII. How Non-Financial Types Can Use This Knowledge

You may not see how all of this will be of any use to you. You may not be a "financial type." You may be a "people person." You read this book because an instructor or a boss required it, or because you had only an idle interest in what "financial types" do. How can any of the ideas in this book help you?

Having some basic conversance with finance can be useful in a range of non-financial jobs. There is an infinite variety of these, but a few examples will give you a flavor.

The Marketer

You are selling something. You pitch the item's features and advantages. You may compare it competitors. You might even argue that it can save the customer money versus the status quo. But many customers will be asking some version of: "How does the rate of return I will earn on this item compare with my best alternative?" That is, does your product offer the customer a positive NPV?

"Return" may be more revenue, or savings (lower costs)—they have the same effect on the customer's profitability. Without financial literacy, all you can do is fake it. With this knowledge, plus some data, your argument can be persuasive, answering the most important question your prospective customer will ask.

This sales scenario applies in a very wide range of situations. You may literally be selling cars, say to the manager of a company fleet. You may be selling air conditioning equipment to an office building owner. You may be a college admissions officer trying to convince a parent to send their kid to your expensive university. You may be an advertising agency director persuading your client to spend millions on an ad campaign. **Ultimately, every decision that expends resources should be evaluated in terms of its return**.

The Human Resources Officer

You work in your company's HR department. Line managers complain about high turnover: employees are not equipped with the skills they need to succeed, so many quit or are fired. Retraining their replacements costs a lot of money, which is often wasted if the trainees leave soon thereafter. You want to propose a new program to offer additional skills training to new employees, to improve retention.

The CEO likes the idea in theory, but questions its high cost. You will be much more persuasive if you can quantify your program's benefits that will offset its costs.

The Health Care Provider

You are a physical therapist. You had the good fortune to secure a contract with a large employer, to provide services to its employees at their work site. Your client is considering ending your contract to cut expenses. You show that employees who use your service have 5% lower absenteeism and 3% greater productivity at work, so your contract has a significant NPV. This is much more persuasive than "but the employees are happier!" which is all your competitors can say.

The Politician

You are an elected official, or on the staff of one. You wish to persuade your fellow legislators or the voters that your proposed program will benefit the public far more than its expected cost. Your critics will point out that the costs are immediate and the benefits come later. But if you can estimate your program's NPV—or equivalently, its benefit/cost ratio—and explain it persuasively, you have a massive advantage over the purely political types.

Qualitative arguments are all that non-quantitative people have. If you can quantify—and defend your estimates convincingly—you can dominate a debate.

The Journalist

Finance and businesspeople act like a priesthood: they deliberately use jargon that excludes rather than includes. Many journalists are bamboozled by sexy-sounding buzzwords. If you have some financial literacy, you will have an easier time decoding the obscure code, and spotting charlatans.

Anyone in the information business is basically telling stories, so the above applies whether you are a journalist, a blogger, a documentary producer, or a YouTube host.

The Individual Investor

You probably realize that the automatic savings plans imposed on you—mainly Social Security—will not produce a comfortable lifestyle in retirement. In addition, you are on your own to save enough for any other goals: car, house down payment, vacation, or kids' college.

Financial knowledge can arm you to be a better investor. Chances are, you will begin by investing mainly in stock index funds, which is absolutely correct, and may be enough to meet your needs. But if you ever contemplate managing your own investments, you may wish to become a value investor, as most of the great long-term investors have been. Value investors estimate a stock's intrinsic value—PV again—and wait for emotions to drive the market price below it. Very few investors can to do this; you will be able to.

Conclusion

This book will not make you a financial genius. But it has given you a good start. We stayed at a 50,000-foot level, emphasizing a handful of fundamental concepts. The greater your financial ambitions, the further you will need to press beyond this book's introduction. You may find returning here occasionally will help you stay oriented.

Finance pervades all important decisions about allocating resources. For a few readers, these skills may be the gateway to continuing self-education that allows you to become quite wealthy. For the rest, this book can help you maintain your competitive edge over other workers in your field, so that your job is the last to be automated away.

Good luck!

G Glossary

Specialized terms are defined and interpreted here. Note that the interpretations are quite subjective.

Active management: Mutual funds whose managers actively attempt to choose issues so their fund's performance exceeds its benchmark, usually an index.

Alpha: A measure of average investment return compared to a benchmark such as the market average. Active investment managers seek to generate alpha—few do.

Arbitrage: Purchasing something in one market and selling it at a higher price in a different market. The opportunities to arbitrage cause prices to converge across markets.

Assets: Items of value that a firm owns, which generally increase the value of the firm.

Balance sheet: Summary of a firm's assets and liabilities at a point in time, to produce its net worth.

Basis point: One-one hundredth of one percent, i.e., .01%. Sometimes abbreviated 'bps'

BDC (business development corporation): Lender to small and mid-sized businesses, often at floating rates of interest.

Benchmark: A threshold for comparison, most commonly of investment returns. Benchmarks should be relevant to the investment being compared: stocks should be compared to a stock index like the S&P 500, and bonds to a bond index.

Beta: A measure of a stock's volatility relative to the market as a whole. A beta of less than 1.0 may be associated with a stable company like an electric utility. A beta well above 1.0 may signify a volatile growth company such as a biotech firm.

Book value: A company's net worth, from its balance sheet. Because some components of the balance sheet are counted very conservatively, net worth is often far less than the company's market capitalization.

Business cycle: Periodic increases and decreases in economic activity (GDP).

(Share) Buybacks: The purchase by a company of outstanding shares from shareholders to reduce the share count and make each remaining share more valuable.

Capital Assets Pricing Model (CAPM): Framework for classifying investments by their risk and return, measuring their relative riskiness (**beta**) and their systematic over- or under-performance relative to the market (**alpha**).

Capital gains: The difference between the selling price of an asset and its original purchase price.

Capital expenditures (capex): Purchases by a firm of assets with expected life of more than one year.

Capital structure: The mix of types of financing a corporation uses: **debt, equity**, and various types of each. See also **leverage**

Cashflow: The actual cash that enters or leaves a firm. This is slightly different from accounting earnings because the latter includes noncash expenses such as depreciation, and may "mark to market" changes in the market (paper) value of investments.

Cashflow diagram: A timeline showing cash flowing it no and out of an investment, with expenditures shown as negative cashflows and returns shown as positive cashflows. Cashflow diagrams are extremely helpful in preparing an financial analysis.

Competition policy: Authority for government to maintain competition. Called antitrust policy in the United States.

Competitive advantage: The dimension on which a firm is superior to its competitors—cost, quality, expertise, or logistical efficiency.

Competitive moat: Results of company efforts to preclude competitors from attracting their customers. Moats are especially durable competitive advantages.

Consumer Price Index (CPI): Index of overall prices paid by consumers; the basic measure of inflation.

Consumption: Spending that doesn't produce a positive financial **return**—it has insufficient positive cashflows to counterbalance its costs (negative cashflow). If you take a course purely for your enjoyment, it's consumption. If you use the knowledge to increase your income, the course was an **investment**.

Correlation: Measure of the relationship between two variables. Oil Company A's stock price may be closely positively correlated with Oil Company B's, since common forces (oil prices) affect both: their correlation will be almost 1.0. By contrast, an oil company and an airline may be highly negatively correlated, with a correlation coefficient of close to -1.0. Choosing portfolio components that are little correlated can dampen the portfolio's **volatility**.

Correlation coefficient: measure of the statistical relationship between two variables, ranging from -1.0 to +1.0. If two items move in the same direction they are positively correlated, and negative if they move in opposite directions. Zero indicates no apparent relationship. Portfolios comprised of uncorrelated positions can dampen volatility at little cost in performance (return).

Cost of capital: The return a firm must offer investors to attract capital. This is usually set by the best alternative of similar risk available to investors. See also **weighted average cost of capital**. Cost of capital sets a firm's discount rate in evaluating investment projects.

Coupon rate: A bond's annual payment of interest, as a percentage of par. If a bind paid a $50 interest payment each year on a bond whose par value is $1,000, that is a 5% coupon rate.

Debt: Borrowing, either to fund a new investment or to cover consumption (i.e., a **deficit**).

Debt to equity ratio: The ratio of a firm's outstanding debt to its stockholders' equity. A crude indication of **leverage**.

Deficit Remainder of expenses after subtracting income. Running a deficit means the firm is spending more than its revenues. See also **surplus**.

Differentiation: Persuading customers your product is different and superior (offering them a **value proposition**) so you can charge prices higher than your competitors.

Discounting: Adjusting future payments to account for the time value of money, converting them into **present values**.

Discounted cashflow (DCF): Method of valuing stocks that incorporates both projected dividends and capital gains/losses by discounting each.

Discount rate (DR): The **opportunity cost** of funds, usually expressed as an annual rate, used to convert **future values to present values**.

Diversification: Distributing your resources over multiple projects, assets, or industries. Diversification—up to a point—lowers individual position risk, but it cannot eliminate market (or systematic) risk.

Dividend: Payment by the firm to its shareholders (usually quarterly) out of current earnings.

Dividend discount model: Method of valuing stock that discounts the stream of projected future dividends.

Duration: Time until half of a bond's positive cashflows have been distributed to the investor. Duration is computed as a weighted average of the individual discounted cashflows. It is also a crude measure of how responsive a bond's price is to changes in interest rates: longer-duration bonds' prices will swing more when rates change.

Efficient Market Hypothesis (EMH): If new information on an investment (such as the success or failure of a new product) quickly translates into changes in the investment's price, the market is efficient. Different scholars disagree about the degree of efficiency of different markets, so there are several versions of the EMH of varying strength.

Enterprise value: A firm's market capitalization plus debt outstanding. A broader measure of corporate valuation than market cap alone, it facilitates comparisons across firms with different **capital structures**.

Equity: (Partial) ownership of a firm, usually by shares of common stock. On a firms' balance sheet, equity is the firm's net worth. Stockholders fall behind debtholders in liquidation, so their investment is riskier and commands a **risk premium**.

ETF (exchange traded fund): A variant on mutual funds that trade like stocks. ETFs originally had significantly lower costs than **mutual funds**, but over the past twenty years as their market share expanded, their cost advantage mostly eroded.

Fixed costs: Costs that do not vary with quantity produced (scale). Often these are start-up costs.

Future value: The contemporary-year value of a **cashflow** (payment or expense) before **discounting** to convert to **present value**.

Growth: Change in any amount, such as prices or quantity. A rate of change is defined as: [New amount – old amount] / Old amount.

Growth investing: Investing on stocks based mainly on earnings growth. Contrast with **value investing**.

Hurdle rate: The rate of return a candidate project must "hurdle over" to be approved. This is usually the decisionmaker's **cost of capital**.

Indexing: Mutual funds and ETFs that do not attempt to beat their benchmarks, but only to match it. They buy and hold all issues in their index.

Industry: Collection of firms selling a similar product or service.

Inflation: General rise in prices. Measured by changes in the Consumer Price Index (CPI).

Internal rate of return (IRR): The **discount rate (DR)** at which a project's NPV equals zero. This is often compared to a **hurdle rate**, with the project approved if the IRR exceeds the hurdle rate.

Income statement: Summary of the firm's costs and revenues in a given time period, to produce its profits.

Investment Activities that generate more positive cashflow than they cost (negative cashflow).

Leverage: Commonly, the use of debt to buy an asset. For example, a homeowner with a mortgage has used other people's money to buy the house. The owner's returns are magnified because they only invested their down payment, yet they enjoy all of the change in the price of the house: they are "leveraged." More generally, leverage means taking on a fixed cost to lower your variable costs or increase your returns.

Liabilities: Obligations of a firm. These are subtracted from assets in a firm's **balance sheet** to compute its net worth.

Liquidation: Process to disestablish a failing firm and sell off its assets, to return at least partial capital to its investors. Debt holders receive first priority and shareholders last priority.

Liquidity: A liquid asset is cash, or can be converted to cash quickly and at little cost. You cannot spend stock at the grocery store: it must be converted into a liquid form such as cash.

Margin: In business terms, margin is profits divided by revenues, establishing how profitable a firm is. In economics terms, "at the margin" relates to one more unit produced or purchased.

Market capitalization (market cap): The total value of a company, as reflected in the stock market. Literally, number of shares outstanding x current price per share.

Market share: Company revenues divided by total sales in the market.

Master Limited Partnership (MLP): A business form that invests in energy assets. Like REITs and BDCs, MLPs are exempt from corporate taxes if they pay at least 90% of their earnings to owners/

Moat: See **competitive moat**.

Modern Portfolio Theory (MPT): Principles of portfolio design to optimize the portfolio's combination of risk and return.

Momentum investing: Investing in stocks based on recent price trends, expecting them to continue.

Monopolistic competition: A form of oligopoly in which each firm "locks in" their customers to create a de facto monopoly. See also **competitive moat**.

Mutual funds Portfolios that pool the capital of many retail investors to purchase assets collectively. There are roughly 10,000 different funds investing in a very wide range of asset classes, regions, and industries. A basic distinction is whether a fund is **actively** or **passively** managed.

Net present value (NPV): The amount of value an investment adds to a company or portfolio. It is the difference between the **present value** of the investment's positive (benefits) and negative (costs) **cashflows**.

Net worth: The net value of a company's assets (what it owns) after subtracting its liabilities (what it owes). The company's shareholders collectively control its new worth.

Nominal: Unadjusted for inflation.

Opportunity cost: The opportunities foregone by committing a scarce resource, such as time or capital.

Optimize: To choose a combination of decision variables that maximizes an objective, subject to constraints. For example, an investment manager may wish to maximize his expected return while keeping risk below a ceiling, or minimize risk while keeping return above a floor.

Passive management: See **indexing**.

Payout policy: A firm's choice regarding returning capital to shareholders, either through **dividends** or share **buybacks**.

Payout ratio: The share of earnings paid out in dividends.

Plowback ratio: 1 – payout ratio. The share of earnings retained by the firm.

Portfolio: A collection of assets. The portfolio's **return** is the weighted average of each asset's return.

Present value: The value of a future payment, **discounted** to reflect the time value of money. For a payment N years in the future, PV = FV / (1 + DR) ^N

Pricing power: Ability to raise prices without suffering a significant decline in sales. This is another way of saying the firm enjoys customers with low price elasticity of demand.

Profit Revenue minus costs—the goal of any for profit business.

Profitability index: a measure of the "bang" an investment project offers per "buck" of cost. Literally, profitability index is NPV/Cost.

Real: Adjusted for inflation. A real rate of return is the nominal rate minus the inflation rate.

Realized gain or loss: An investor who continues to hold an asset whose price has changed has experienced only a paper gain or loss. The change doesn't become real until it is realized by selling the asset. Most taxes on capital gains are not levied until those gains are realized.

REIT (real estate investment trust): REITs are collections of property owned by a group of shareholders, similar to a mutual fund. Most REITs specialize in a general type of property such as shopping centers, hospitals, or multifamily homes. REITs receive favorable corporate tax treatment like BDCs and MLPs.

Return (on investment, ROI): The ratio of benefits earned to the investment's cost, usually expressed as a percentage.

Return on equity: Ratio of net income (earnings) to the company's equity (net worth). A measure of how efficiently the firm uses equity investment.

Return on invested capital: Ratio of net income (earnings) to all of the company's paid-in capital: debt and equity. A measure of the company's capital efficiency.

Returns to scale: Trajectory of returns as a function of quantity of productions (scale). The typical distinction is among increasing, decreasing, or constant returns to scale.

Revenue: Gross amount earned from the sale of products. Equals quantity sold x price.

Risk premium: The additional return above that of a riskless asset that a risky asset must offer to attract investors.

Rule of 72: Shortcut for estimating compounding of an asset. The number of years the asset will need to double in value is [72 / growth rate (ignoring %)]. Therefore, the growth rate to achieve a doubling in a given number of years is [72/years]. The Rule of 72 can be used for any change in asset value that is a factor of 2: for instance, 4 is 2^2; 8 is 2^3, and 1000 is roughly 2^10.

Savings: Portion of income not consumed. Savings provides the capital for **investment**.

Scenario: set of assumptions about the future that will affect an investments cashflows. Multiple scenarios are used in **sensitivity analysis**

Sector: Group of similar industries.

Sensitivity analysis: Examination of how sensitive an investment recommendation is to future uncertainties. Common performed by estimating NPV under multiple **scenarios**.

Sharpe ratio: Measure of risk-adjusted return: An asset's risk premium (average return minus the risk free rate) divided by its standard deviation. The Sharpe ratio broadly indicates how well you are being compensated for taking risk. Only rare investments have Sharpe ratios above 1.0.

Standard deviation: Measure of variability of a statistic: the square root of its **variance**.

Surplus: Positive difference between income and expenses. Surpluses are necessary to make resources available to pay debt principal.

Tax: Involuntary (mandatory) payment to government, sometimes intended to discourage the taxed behavior.

Total return: An asset's total return includes **dividends** and **capital gains**.

Value Investing: Investing in stocks based on mainly on low prices. Contrast with **growth investing**.

Value proposition: The implicit offer a firm makes to its customers to justify its price. Value propositions are especially important if the firm's offering is not the lowest price.

Variable costs: Costs that vary with scale. The next increment of variable costs is known as marginal cost.

Variance: Measure of the volatility of a statistic, measured as the sum of the absolute values of each observation's value minus the mean of all observations.

Volatility: Degree and frequency of change, usually applied to an asset's returns. Bonds' coupons aren't at all volatile—that's why they are known as "fixed income." Stocks' returns are more so, with blue chip companies the least volatile among stocks, and small cap firms the most volatile.

Weighted average cost of capital A firm's capital cost, combining its **debt** and its **equity**, weighted for their respective proportions in the firm's **capital structure.**

Working capital: Funds needed to buy short-lived assets such as inventory needed for ongoing operations. Distinct from **capital expenditures** (capex)

Yield: In general, the annual return provided by an asset. It usually (but not always) includes only funds received over and above the original investment.

Yield to call: A bond's yield if "called" (redeemed) by the issuer before scheduled maturity.

Yield to maturity: A bond's yield if redeemed by the issuer at its scheduled maturity.

Yield to worst: A bond's yield if "called" (redeemed) by the issuer at the earliest date possible.

Index

About the Author

Philip J. Romero is professor of business administration at the University of Oregon's business school, where he has served as dean. His earlier career includes periods in government economic policymaking as chief economist to the governor of California, in corporate strategy for the chairman of United Technologies Corp., and in national security at the RAND Corp. Romero is a consultant on the economic and competitiveness impacts of proposed policies, a frequent guest on international news programs, and a columnist.

Other Books by Philip J. Romero

The Winner's Toolkit: Competitive Strategies That Real Businesspeople Can Use, Sentia Publishing, Fall 2017

*Hedge Fund Secrets: An Introduction to Quantitative Portfolio Managemen*t (with Tucker Balch), Business Expert Press, Fall 2017

It's the **Income**, *Stupid! The 7 Secrets of a Stress-Free Retirement* (with Riaan Nel), Post Hill Press, Feb. 2017

How Competition Works, Sentia Publishing, Sept. 2016

Health Financing Without Deficits: Reform That Sidesteps Political Gridlock (with Randy S. Miller), Business Expert Press, July 2016

What Hedge Funds Really Do: An Introduction to Portfolio Management (with Tucker Balch), Business Expert Press, Sept. 2014

Your Macroeconomic Edge: Investing Strategies for the Post-Recession World, Business Expert Press, Jan. 2012

Made in United States
Orlando, FL
05 November 2026

90241339R00085